THE BEGGAR III

*False Ego: The Greatest Enemy
of the Spiritual Leader*

B.T. Swami

HARI-NAMA PRESS

First printing 2002

Cover and interior design by Subala / Ecstatic Creations
Photography by Adam and Christine Kenney

Printed in the United States of America

ISBN 1-885414-10-2

Persons interested in the subject matter of this book are
invited to correspond with the publisher:

Hari-Nama Press
PO Box 76451, Washington, DC 20013
(800) 949-5333 US • (301) 765-8155 outside US
Fax: (301) 765-8157
hpress@compuserve.com

Other works by
B.T. Swami
(Swami Krishnapada)

The Beggar I
*Meditations and Prayers on
the Supreme Lord*

The Beggar II
Crying Out for the Mercy

Spiritual Warrior I
Uncovering Spiritual Truths in Psychic Phenomena

Spiritual Warrior II
Transforming Lust into Love

Spiritual Warrior III
Solace for the Heart In Difficult Times

Leadership for an Age of
Higher Consciousness
Administration from a Metaphysical Perspective

Dedication

I dedicate this book to all spiritual mentors, as you struggle daily

in checking the false ego so the divine ego can fully surface.

I pray this book will be a helpful companion on this

difficult but exciting journey.

Contents

Acknowledgments

I would like to once again thank Stewart Cannon

for his spectacular work on the cover, artwork

and layout and Christine Kenney for taking

the photos used in the inside artwork.

I would also like to thank Jason Gerick,

Palak Patel, John Fitch, Anita Kodwin,

Missy Lewellyn, Prentiss Alter and Michael Buhler

for transcribing numerous tapes, and

Raga Makeda Cannon, Joslin Morgan,

Krista Helfer and Adam Kenney for their

careful editing of the text.

2   *The Beggar III*

Editor's Preface

The Beggar series is a collection of meditations and reflections written and shared over the years by His Holiness Bhakti-Tirtha Swami, the world's only African-American *guru* in the Vaishnava tradition. Although new to the Western world, the Vaishnava tradition, brought primarily to the West by His Divine Grace A.C. Bhaktivedanta Swami Prabhupada, has been handed down in an unbroken line from teacher to student for over five thousand years.

One of the principal texts of the Vaishnava tradition is the Bhagavad-gita, a transcript of a conversation between the Lord and His devotee, the great general Arjuna. During the course of this conversation, the Lord explains that the ultimate goal of life and the true source of lasting happiness is to be reunited in loving devotional service with Him and His associates. The Lord goes on to explain that, simply out of His love for the living entities, He occasionally descends or sends messengers to remind us of our higher calling. Although the names may change—Christ, Allah, Krishna, Jehovah, Yahweh—and there may be some external "religious" differences based on the culture being addressed, the fundamental message is always the same: Continuous loving service to the Lord, expressed in this lifetime by how we serve and care for each other.

Bhakti-Tirtha Swami makes several references to the Bhagavad-gita and other Vedic literatures in the course of these meditations, in some cases speaking to us as if calling out from within the pastimes themselves. While an understanding of Vedic literature does enhance the reading experience, these meditations are definitely not meant exclusively for those in the Vaishnava tradition. Anyone who has ever struggled to persevere on the spiritual path, or whose life has been touched by the causeless love and compassion of a genuine spiritual guide will identify with these meditations and find a new appreciation of why and how this guidance has come.

His Holiness addresses the Lord using many different names from the Vedas, to emphasize different moods and relationships between the soul and the Lord—just as the names "Mr. Smith" "Daddy" and "The Boss" may refer to the same person, but illustrate different relationships between the speaker and the subject. We have provided a glossary at the end of the text that includes brief definitions of these names and other terms from the Vedas that may be unfamiliar.

We are very pleased to have the opportunity to share this third set of meditations in *The Beggar* series, and we wish all of our readers a renewed faith in the love and the mercy of the Lord, as they flow to us through the compassionate messengers we know as *guru.*

Foreword

We are all born into this world with at least five senses that we come to recognize and rely on as we grow and develop perceptions and memories based on those five senses. Memories and perceptions are further influenced by added instructions from trusted parents and elders, and others who would influence what we should think, say and do.

Very early in our lives we get the perceptions and conclusions that we are independent, separate beings, and want to be in charge of the choices and directions of our lives.

We soon realize that we have this thing called the mind that talks to us constantly, and supports us in our individuality and our efforts to get what we desire as individuals. We become aware that what we can perceive with our five senses as "me" is our body. Some call this ego, or "body-mind" or "me mind." We falsely and mistakenly believe that this is who we really are. When things don't turn out the way we want them to, this collection of beliefs, experiences, and desires brings all of its doubts, fears, frustrations, ravings and ranting to bear to convince us that we must still listen to it, and keep it in charge, because it is real and the only thing that we can trust. Once in a while, something inside so strong manages to remind us that something greater than we are is inside and around us, and it needs to be listened to, especially when we don't know what to do, or where to turn for advice and guidance.

Now comes John E. Favors who tells us who he was before he became this internationally known and revered spiritual leader now known as His Holiness Bhakti-tirtha Swami Krishnapada. Bhakti-tirtha Swami talks and writes to leaders around the world on servant leadership (see *Leadership for an Age of Higher Consciousness*), and to individuals about the challenges that face us all in his *Spiritual Warrior* series of books. Bhakti-tirtha Swami loves us enough to share his most intimate and painful prayers and meditations to his spiritual master, teachers, and the common CREATOR of us all in his series of books called *The Beggar*.

In this latest book, *The Beggar III: False Ego—The Greatest Enemy of the Spiritual Leader*, Bhakti-tirtha Swami deliberately presents himself as being subject to the same fears, doubts, and self-inflicted anguish that we experience as the false ego (me mind) continues to try to convince us that it is all there is, and that we are hopeless and helpless in the face of the major challenges facing all of us in the world today. But wait! In the answers to his prayers and meditations, we experience the wisdom, love and "causeless mercy" that are always there to guide us if we ask earnestly and honestly to be led in service to the Godhead.

Bhakti-tirtha Swami courageously and humbly lets us in on his false ego's chatter as he meditates and waits for his false ego to become quiet enough for him to hear his higher Self or Soul and the advice of his spiritual masters. Bhakti-tirtha Swami's revealing of his inner conversations, begging, meditations and prayers is most helpful because he helps us, the readers, to realize that we are not alone in our struggles with the false ego. These struggles are part of our humanity, and make us stronger as we bow down and listen to our higher self's God consciousness (Krishna consciousness, Christ consciousness, etc.). The great works that Bhakti-tirtha Swami has been able to perform worldwide testify to the value of rising above the attacks of the false ego and the notion that we are defined by our body. We must all find a way to live and act out of love, using our life energy to move toward our greatest potential and highest good, and teach by loving example that we can share that love with others—unconditionally, as does the CREATOR.

I find this struggle to be a daunting process as my false ego seems so persistently powerful and clever at finding ways to insert itself between me and the higher Self that I know is there. Trusting the process seems to be my biggest challenge. This challenge must be overcome if we are to be leaders in raising the collective consciousness, elevate our own consciousness and learn to love, and love to learn. *The Beggar III* is a gift of love to help us in our struggle. We will realize the magnitude of this gift as we trust the process of surrender, prayer and meditation, and as we follow the teachings of this powerful spiritual leader and the books, tapes and speeches he shares with us. *The Beggar III* will make us think, and, more importantly, help us grow toward the perfection that the CREATOR so lovingly and graciously gave to each of us.

It was in response to Bhakti-tirtha Swami's openness, honesty, and non-proselytizing spiritual leadership that I had the pleasure of inviting him to speak to my colleagues at the National Medical Association Convention. I have also enjoyed his gracious visits to the studio of WEAA-FM radio (88.9FM) in Baltimore, Maryland to share his wisdom as a guest on my radio show Healthline 2010. Bhakti-tirtha Swami has consented to come into the studio as each of his books has been published to interact with my two-way talk audience.

Bhakti-tirtha Swami's books are all written to facilitate us in keeping our highest Self in charge of our lives as we move toward our greatest potential and highest good. The Beggar III is his latest contribution to helping us do the often-difficult inner work of understanding that our life force is our God force. Typical of all true leaders, he teaches by loving, living example. I beg you to join us in the process!

Love, Inner Peace, and Optimal Health
John T. Chissell, M.D.
Author: *Pyramids of Power*

Author's Notes

    There are ten common types of Vaishnava prayers. These ten forms have been used by many of the great *acharyas*. Srila Narottama Dasa Thakura particularly mentions these in his book titled *Prarthana*, and these same prayers were practically all exhibited in the writings of Srila Bhaktivinoda Thakura. I have written *The Beggar* series using these ten types of prayerful statements, which are described below:

1. **Samprarthanatmika:** Words of direct prayer to the Lord.

2. **Sva-dainya-bodhika:** Words informing the Lord of one's own humility.

3. **Manah-siksa:** Instructions to one's own mind.

4. **Vilapatmika:** Statements of extreme lamentation.

5. **Vaisnava-mahima-prakasika:** Statements revealing the glories of the Lord's devotees.

6. **Sri-guru-vaisnave-vijnapti-rupa:** Supplications made to one's spiritual master, or to the devotees of the Lord.

7. Sri-dhama-vase-lipsatmika: Statements revealing the desire to live in the holy places of the Lord's pastimes.

8. Sadhaka-deher-lalasa-sucika: Prayers revealing desires to execute regulated devotional service in the body of a practicing devotee.

9. Siddha-deher-lalasamayi: Prayers revealing desires to execute spontaneous devotional service in the perfect spiritual body.

10. Aksepa-bodhika: Prayers revealing intense grief and sorrow in which one blames oneself for falling into the material world.

"False ego means accepting this body as oneself. When one understands that he is not his body and is spirit soul, he comes to his real ego. Ego is there. False ego is condemned, but not real ego. In the Vedic literature *(Brhad-aranyaka Upanisad 1.4.10)* it is said, *aham brahmasmi:* I am Brahman, I am spirit. This 'I am,' the sense of self, also exists in the liberated stage of self-realization. This sense of 'I am' is ego, but when the sense of 'I am' is applied to this false body it is false ego. When the sense of self is applied to reality, that is real ego. There are some philosophers who say we should give up our ego, but we cannot give up our ego, because ego means identity. We ought, of course, to give up the false identification with the body."

(Bhagavad Gita 13 8-12 purport)

"The *mahat-tattva* is the via medium between pure spirit and material existence. It is the junction of matter and spirit wherefrom the false ego of the living entity is generated. All living entities are differentiated parts and parcels of the Personality of Godhead. Under the pressure of false ego, the conditioned souls, although parts and parcels of the Supreme Personality of Godhead, claim to be the enjoyers of material nature. This false ego is the binding force of material existence. The Lord again and again gives a chance to the bewildered conditioned souls to get free from this false ego, and that is why the material creation takes place at intervals. He gives the conditioned souls all facilities for rectifying the activities of the false ego, but He does not interfere with their small independence as parts and parcels of the Lord."

(Srimad Bhagavatam 3.5.28 purport)

"Any inattentiveness or carelessness may cause falldown. This falldown is due to false ego. From the status of pure consciousness, the false ego is born because of misuse of independence. We cannot argue about why false ego arises from pure consciousness. Factually, there is always the chance that this will happen, and therefore one has to be very careful. False ego is the basic principle for all material activities, which are executed in the modes of material nature. As soon as one deviates from pure God consciousness, he increases his entanglement in material reaction. The entanglement of materialism is the material mind, and from this material mind, the senses and material organs become manifest."

(SB 3.26.23-24 purport)

THE BEGGAR III

*False Ego: The Greatest Enemy
of the Spiritual Leader*

*"My false ego jumped up
and down clapping. 'You are my hero,
for you are a first class associate!'"*

Meditation 1

Denying the false ego is a sign of a big false ego

My false ego greeted me heartily: "Welcome to a new millennium. I thank you for being so supportive in the past, and I look forward to even more of your support in this new era."

I did not recognize this stranger or understand what he was referring to. I had neither the time nor interest to be concerned. After all, so many students and admirers of mine were waiting to have my audience. As I ignored him, my false ego jumped up and down clapping: "You are such a first class associate," he beamed at me.

My first student entered my office to see me. He was bright-eyed, shy and youthful. "Dear Master," he inquired after bowing to me. "How can I become more appreciative of the Vedic teachings explained to us by Srila Prabhupada and various great acaryas?" I replied: "Simply read very conscientiously, at least one or two hours a day. Read in the mood that you will have to explain what you read to others."

As the student left, I thought to myself, "do I read Vedic literatures in such a scrutinizing way every day? Of course not. I am far too busy explaining to others that their greatest stumbling block is that they do not study the sacred texts and scriptures." My false ego jumped up and down clapping, while saying: "You are such a first class associate."

A second student entered my midst. "Master, I am having so much trouble controlling my sex life with my wife. What can I do?"

I replied: "Stop lusting after her body and learn to love her soul. Love how she chants, how she cooks, serves the Deities, and takes care of your children. Love how she dresses so chastely; love her compassionate smile. Love how she so graciously cares for all Vaishnavas. Love how eager she is to see and hear you preach. When you look into her eyes, understand her joy and pain. And when she cries, love her even more for her amazing tolerance."

As he was leaving, I thought: "Why do my householders think I am a marriage counselor?" My false ego jumped up and down clapping. "You are my hero, for you are a first class associate!"

A renounced student came in next. He bowed down low and took some time getting up. "Master," he said, now on his knees: "How can I maintain celibacy, mentally and physically?"

Without batting an eye, I replied: "Always be selective about what you see and hear and who you associate with. Control your tongue! Watch what you say and what you eat. Keep the mind enthusiastically engaged. Do not be frivolous with women. Always be mission-conscious. Live simply with detachment."

Before the next person came in, I spoke to myself out loud, "When will these simple students learn to connect from the heart in all relationships the way I always do? When will they, like me, approach all encounters from the heart and not from their minds, intelligence, tongue or genitals?"

My false ego jumped up and down clapping. "You are the finest of associates. Where else could I find such a first class companion?"

Just then, a pair of my married students entered the room. "Swami, we're having so much trouble raising our twenty-one-year-old son and nineteen-year-old daughter." I replied quickly, to keep them from droning on too long. "Now that your children are young adults, do not treat them like they are yours but instead also become their friends. As you guide and instruct them, spend more time trying to understand their needs and perceptions. Show them you will always be there for each of them and fully honor their individuality."

When the couple left, I thought: "Those two are so dysfunctional themselves, it will be a miracle for them to raise sound-minded, spiritually healthy children."

My false ego practically danced a jig. "Bravo hero, bravo. May I learn to think and behave like you, for you are the finest of associates!"

"Guru Maharaja," my next student spoke softly and humbly. "Please instruct me how I can chant better rounds."

My reply was swift and ingenious. "Avoid the ten offenses. Chant with desperation and humility. See your chanting as an internal 'fax line' to connect with Guru and the Divine Couple. Be attentive and try to finish your chanting during the early morning hours."

He began to ask for further clarification, but I stopped him. "I'm sorry. I'd talk a bit longer but I still have ten rounds to finish and the time is getting toward late evening." "What a first class associate," my false ego applauded. "Who can predict the wondrous things you'll say and do?"

Yet another student came in to interrupt my pure chanting. This one asked how he could personally take more shelter of praying. "We must never pray in a demanding way," I reminded him. "Our position is to serve the Supreme Lord—not to request his service."

He seemed quickly satisfied. So, enjoying the sound of my own voice, I elaborated a bit on the message. "If we do everything very mindfully, then everything we do is a prayer. Once we get to this stage, we can live completely free from doubt that the Lord is hearing us. The Lord is hearing us. But never think that we can hear His reply. Remember, the mind and intelligence are capable of playing many tricks on us. They'll make fools of us without our knowing it."

This student was more attentive than the others. He seemed to listen so raptly that I couldn't help embellishing further. "There are ten types of prayers that we Vaishnavas make," I said to him, and then pompously described each one in detail.

"Should I practice one or all types of these prayers Gurudeva?"

Suddenly my tone grew agitated. "Haven't you read my books? In these brilliant works, I have thoroughly explained these ten types of prayers."

He held his head down in shame.

"Writing these books has taken up so much of my valuable time. Why are you not reading and appreciating them?" I asked, dismissing him with a grimace.

My false ego applauded like a madman. "You are such a first class associate; I am honored to be linked with you."

Next, a few senior students came in to see me and express their gratitude for my instruction. "Master you are so kind, patient and tolerant. Everyday you engage in writing books, answering all of your correspondence and preaching in so many dangerous environments. You work both globally and locally, and you deal patiently with so many of the devotees' personal problems. You are so dear to us, and so empowering. "

I smiled, thinking to myself: "What great austerities they must have done in a previous life to get my association. Do they even realize how fortunate and blessed they are to know and serve me?" Just as I was thinking this, one of them interrupted. "What is the secret of your great success, Swami?"

"It is all due to the mercy of my Guru and Krishna."

My false ego stood up for my command performance, giving thunderous applause. "I do not deserve your association! They say that no one should take sannyas in the Age of Quarrel and Hypocrisy, but you have used your ashram so expertly. You are the master manipulator; Kali Yuga's finest. I beg you, please teach me what you know."

This time I looked closer at this uncultured entity. Stars, crowd-pleasers, like me pick up all kinds of strange fans and admirers. I wondered what he thinks we have in common and why he thinks I would even give him the time of day. Actually, I have no idea who he is or what his agenda is. But I will say this about him: He has very good taste in hero-mentors, or as he calls me "associates." And besides that, for some reason, he has become fortunate enough to desire my company. Maybe he read an article about me in a prestigious journal. Whatever the case, he apparently wants to be guided by me like all my other admirers. So, what can I do? I guess I'll have to find time to mercifully guide him.

"Being so sneaky, however, my false ego is very adept at hiding from us in so many places."

Meditation 2

Searching for the false ego

My soul and intelligence have been informed by my spiritual master that my false ego is proceeding with his plans to destroy us. We know that this is not a rumor as we have received this warning from such a perfect source. Therefore, my soul and intelligence have cleverly decided to seek out the false ego and destroy it before it destroys us. Being so sneaky, however, my false ego is adept at hiding from us in so many places. We don't know exactly where to look for him. Maybe we should wait for him to show himself. Surely, he will appear soon.

While waiting for my false ego to surface, I started reflecting on how special I am as a sannyasi and guru. Just imagine. Here I am, in the highest spiritual order; a distinguished member of the one percent. I have so many disciples the world over. Every day I get letters from them, and they think of me constantly.

The grhasthas are so attached to their household life and all kinds of sense gratification, and most celibate brahmacaris are just a few years away from becoming attached householders. As for babajis, most of them are just material and spiritual misfits. Sannyasa is the real life—a lifestyle fit for the truly mature and qualified.

It's funny. My spiritual master once explained how the false ego could hide in the different ashramas. He said that it can hide in and behind any of the four orders of life, and that no one is a real master of any particular status, other than that of being an eternal servant of Krishna. I don't have the slightest idea what my spiritual master meant by this, or why he mentioned it to me. Do you?

As I continued to sit and wait for my false ego to surface, I started pondering how my mother organization ISKCON is the only true society in the world. All other religions and philosophies are false and have absolutely no value. A person who is not in ISKCON hasn't the slightest chance of ever meeting God. These poor fools don't even know His name is Krishna. Even if someone is a Vaishnava, if he is not worshipping Krishna in Vrndavan under the exalted banner of ISKCON, he is simply useless.

All over the planet, there are so many fallen people and pseudo religionists following so-called *bona-fide* paths. Not to mention all of the showbottle Vaishnavas. It saddens me to see their predicament. Don't these neophytes even realize that only Srila Prabhupada's ISKCON Vaishnavas can go to Krishna?

I am so proud to be a member of ISKCON. After all, we have all the answers, even though we often don't apply them. At least we are not fallen and useless like all those misled fools on other paths.

Of course I am not clear on all of these nuances my spiritual master made. He often gave us seemingly irrelevant instructions. He once explained to us how Krishna in the Bhagavad-Gita says that Krishna will give Himself to anyone who worships Him with love and devotion. I don't understand why my spiritual master would often quote one sloka that "ultimately everyone is journeying toward the Lord, and as they surrender to Him, He rewards them accordingly." I don't have the slightest idea why Gurudeva bothered us with such rudimentary fundamentals. Do you?

At the moment, I have too many other concerns to figure out that mystery. Actually, I am planning how we can ambush my false ego and destroy him as soon as he surfaces. It shouldn't be overly difficult since I was born an American. You know, we Americans are really God's people! We have longer life spans than people from other countries, bigger houses, bigger cars, bigger universities, and needless to say, we naturally have bigger smiles. People all over the world want to come and live in our homeland of America. Anywhere we travel, when people discover that we are American, they all want to be our friends.

Surely, we will be the first to go back to Godhead. After all, we have so much to contribute there, and we are the ones who know God best, since he has obviously favored us. I just find it rather odd that my guru left behind so many basic instructions. I still remember how he told us that all serious practitioners must avoid identifying with bodily designations or upadis, and that ultimately Krishna can only be known by uninterrupted and unmotivated devotional service. Krishna Himself already said this, so it's quite strange that Guru Maharaja would waste time and paper repeating such a simple instruction. I have no idea why he did. Do you?

Because so much time has passed since we began looking for him, I am sure that my false ego will soon reveal himself so we can once and for all destroy him. Of course, I'm not very worried about catching him. After all, how hard can that be? Because of my excellent karma there is nowhere that I am confined from going, and there are very few restrictions on my person.

Besides, everyone knows that this is a man's world, materially and spiritually. Nearly all the great philosophers, scientists, educators and spiritualists were men. Even God is a man, at least originally. And, while I don't want to rub it in, Maya and Eve were both females. Femininity is the temptation energy, thus it is the feminine principle that degrades society.

That being the case, men should always conspire with one another and make it difficult for women to excel. This is an important service to society, thus, in consideration of the larger framework, we men must make it difficult for women to be recognized, supported and facilitated. Otherwise, if we become too lax, Maya or Dhurga devi and her energy will tempt and influence mankind to fall. We men must be extremely careful, because if women rise too high, they will lower the standard of everything, and possibly even take over.

I regret saying it in his absence, but I do not know why my spiritual master wrote in so many places in His books that we are not these bodies but that we are pure spirit souls, one in quality with God but not in quantity. I do not have the slightest idea what my Gurudeva meant by that, or why he spoke and wrote about it so often. Do you?

In Kali Yuga everything is late or slow to start. I guess that's why my false ego hasn't yet showed up; he's probably indulging in some form of laziness or prajalpa. But I'll patiently wait for him to arrive since I know he will appear any minute now. Besides, since I have been forewarned that he's out to destroy us, I must be alert to always have the upper hand.

With the upper hand, I'll be sure to make the first move and finish him off before he even moves to strike. But with nothing else to do while waiting, I'm inclined to do a little more thinking.

Great devotees like me must never become idle. After all, an idle mind is a devil's workshop and thinking aimlessly has no value. I think maybe I'll ponder life itself. Or maybe I'll narrow it down to people. That is to say, human beings, or, more specifically: the children, the elderly and the brahmins. We covered the weaker sex already, but aside from them, there are no more disturbing categories of people than these particular three. What a nuisance these three types create. Aside from women, it's always one of these three types of people who create the greatest disturbance to society. At least to me, that is.

Whenever I'm trying to contemplate the Absolute and enter into samadhi, a child, an elder or a brahmin comes and disturbs my peace. Just think. Little children are always crying or getting sick. And big children are worse. They wander around like ignorant menaces, demanding all kinds of entertainment and stimulation. The plain fact is, whatever age a child is, he is always making demands. When they're little they just lie around sleeping unproductively, and when they're older they want to play all the time.

Elderly people are not much better. Too old to be productive, they demand everyone's care and attention. And, if you give them a moment to speak they start talking on and on about the old days and everything they did for you, a distant relative or someone else you hardly know or care about.

And don't get me started on brahmins. Most brahmin priests are penniless. Naturally then, they're totally dependent. They rarely have practical skills and can do very little with their hands. You would think that this would make them humble, but no! Brahmins are always wanting to preach, teach or do yajnas and be taken care of just like little children. Frankly, I do not see the value in providing care or protection for any of these four categories of useless people. But for some reason my spiritual master seemed to almost favor them.

I remember him explaining that brahmins, the elderly, women and children are always to be protected in civilized societies. Otherwise, if they were neglected, he said, members of that society's life span would be shortened and their civilization would fall apart. With all the studying I have to do, it's rather peculiar that my guru would bog me down with these trivial considerations. I don't have the slightest idea why he gave such importance to these people. Do you?

I'm getting very bored and tired waiting for my false ego to surface. One day we will have to find him and destroy him, before he becomes too much of a threat. Maybe our staying in one place will give him an advantage and make it easier for him to ambush us. Besides that, when we stay still, it's much too easy for him to evade us. Who knows? Perhaps he has already been killed, or maybe he's still hiding out in fear, aware that we are searching for him to kill him. We had better not drop our guard, because if we do, that is when he is sure to attack.

I hear that the false ego is clever and can hide in unusual places. Sometimes he even enters several places at the same time, and he's so elusive, it's almost as if he has mystic powers. With all of his abilities to travel extensively, he sometimes gets far out of reach, making it very discouraging to look for him. Other times, he comes so close he could destroy us before we even notice him.

Well, my spiritual master told me my false ego is out to destroy my soul and intelligence, but I think that's kind of weird. With so many crazy and dysfunctional people in the world, I don't know why he would attack such a well-adjusted person as me.

Having used every other recourse at my disposal to find him, and being desperate for a new strategy, I think maybe I'll review my guru's other teachings. Somehow I feel if I understood Gurudeva's other remarks, they might offer some clues into my false ego's whereabouts.

Guru Maharaja sometimes used Sanskrit in his instructions. He taught us that his original name, Abhay, means "one who is fearless," and that this name is particularly applicable to those who take shelter at the lotus feet of Lord

Sri Krishna. I would like to think more about the subtle meanings of this and other Sanskrit words, but right now I am in a life-threatening predicament.

Will I find my false ego before he finds me? Can I destroy him before he destroys me? Or am I just wasting my time? Maybe he doesn't even exist or is already dead? Then again, maybe he does exist and has already attacked. Maybe I'm the one who is dying, or the one who needs enlightenment. This is all getting extremely confusing. I can't figure out what the real situation is. Can you?

If only there was just one person on the planet more qualified than me who could enlighten me. The answer is probably in those esoteric translations Gurudeva never got to because he was so focused on giving us fundamentals. Oh well, I guess my false ego won't ever be found. The whole situation is terribly frightening, or maybe my false ego is afraid of me. Can I destroy him before he destroys me? Or is he already destroying me? What do you think?

"*The very thought of living without my false ego was threatening. But in spite of my fear, I watched him pick up his belongings and leave*"

Meditation 3

The false ego was my coach

In a short time in the near future my false ego and I will be parting company, and I greet his departure with mixed feelings. His absence will leave a big void, because he's almost all I have ever known and invested my time in. At the same time, I realize what a fool I've been to keep him as a roommate and close associate. All those times we were spending time together, he seemed to be the best of friends, but now I realize that he was my greatest enemy.

I don't know why it took so long to realize it, but I've finally recognized his wicked patterns. He always intrudes at just the right time to cut me off from real loving connections. He is very clever at convincing me that everyone is my competitor, and that my actual enemies are friends and my real friends are enemies.

Making me suspicious of everyone, my false ego has always convinced me to think that I was at my very best when I was manipulative and duplicitous. When I acted guileless, pleasant and straightforward, he told me I was being foolish and nañve, and setting myself up for heartache.

Being the main ghostwriter of my life story, my false ego always coached me that I should always place my body at the focal point of attention. "Be either first or last," he'd say, "but always be in a visible position. If that means being the most tolerant, then you must totally ingratiate yourself to others and behave like you're the most tolerant. But if it means being the first to speak up or volunteer for an activity, then you must make yourself first, and appear to be the most eager to render service."

When no one else was looking, my false ego would coach me in how to make our point of view heard, either by speaking loudly or by total silence. "After all," he would say, "sometimes there's nothing noisier than silence."

These were the strategies of my false ego, and like a fool I believed every one of his lies and exaggerations. My false ego has lived with me like a shadow for countless lifetimes. We did everything together—we took every meal together, and each of our meals was like a planning session where we would calculate our next maneuver.

As a result of our tenacious teamwork, we eventually achieved amazing worldly results. Anytime I was successful in an area, it was actually my false ego that was responsible. In every endeavor I attempted, my false ego would always enthusiastically coach me on. "You must be the best," he would tell me. "Break records and outdo everyone else if you're going to leave a mark on society."

Like a doting mother, my false ego would never leave me alone. Practically everywhere I went, each project I organized, every event I participated in and every exchange I had with others, my false ego dominated the scene. It is only because of my false ego's inexhaustible diligence that I have collected so many fans and admirers.

In all the places I traveled, people constantly congratulated me on my accomplishment of difficult tasks. They praised me for working vigorously and developing powerful, creative projects. Some were amazed at how often I was available to guide and serve others. If they only knew my real motive, all these people would be shocked to know that it was not really me who was responsible for my victories, rather, it was my false ego that was fully in charge.

Even in politics, my false ego exerted his will. When it was fashionable to be revolutionary, he would recommend I speak radical rhetoric. If it meant being a peacemaker, then I would become the ultimate peacemaker. Even if it meant dressing differently than others just to be sure I wouldn't go unnoticed, he would have me dress eccentrically to catch the public eye. Whenever it profited our sense gratification for me to fit in and dress like others to be accepted and in good standing, then he made sure that I would blend in with nearly anyone.

My false ego's greatest expertise was in the callous judgment of others. Whenever I needed to win popularity by criticizing others, my false ego would have me capture everyone's attention with eloquent criticisms. With elaborate rehearsals, he would teach me how to criticize people in precise rhyme and meter, or, when it was more effective, he'd have me do it just above a whisper. But if conforming to a crowd would better aid our sense gratification, my position on a subject could turn in seconds. With his coaching, I would become the world's most convincing "yes man."

Now I realize that I have been a very obedient slave to my tireless false ego. In fact, he has continuously set me up to fulfill his relentless desires. He used everything at our disposal, namely: my body, senses, mind and intelligence with no regard for my higher interests, needs or feelings.

Due to my false ego's presence, I have behaved like a possessed person whose every action is dictated by a foreigner. Although I've considered myself fully in control, I have actu-

ally been enslaved by the whims of a glutto-
nous false ego. The more I think about our
relationship, the more I realize that this slavery
has created nothing but problems for myself
and other people. Although my false ego has
always convinced me that I am a very special,
high achiever, I see now that my efforts have
actually been counterproductive, because by
refusing to fully serve the Lord's representative, I have failed to serve my truest self-interest.

My false ego has duped me into this terri-
ble predicament as a regular daily affair.
Sometimes he will suggest I do ludicrous things
just to undermine the visibility of others and
put myself back in the center. I do not know
how such an obvious cheater was able to
delude me for so long, but I often hear people
say that those who know us best also know
where to find our subtle weaknesses. My false
ego always capitalized on every weakness in
my nature while convincing me that I should
feel superior to others who don't have a savvy
advisor like him.

I find it so hurtful how my false ego has
crushed me lifetime after lifetime, sabotaging
every opportunity I've had to really grow and
love others without any selfish motive. My
entire existence and every action have been an
offering to my false ego, and the results have
been nothing but painful. You see, no one can
hurt and disappoint you more than those you
deeply trust. Now, I don't know which is
stronger: my anger or my pain.

Just imagine being betrayed by someone

you turn everything over to. Someone you serve so unconditionally and go everywhere with. Imagine being betrayed by that one person you share everything with and reveal your deepest secrets, fears and desires to, only to discover that his only objective was your total enslavement and destruction.

Even worse, now that I've confronted him, my false ego feels no guilt and offers no apologies. Instead, he asks me, "What did you expect? This is my nature. I'm simply that kind of parasite and I never represented myself as anything different."

The funny thing is, I can remember long ago when my false ego and I had so much in common. Since I was previously interested only in prestige, distinction and adoration, we made a wonderful pair and have been partners in crime for lifetimes. But now that I have no interest in the shallow achievements he prods me to, my false ego and I have no true compatibility.

But I must commend him. He has been very thorough and expert at his betrayal. My false ego is such a traitor that when I confront him about his agenda, he accuses me of using him to fulfill my goals. "If you had not had such a cheating, manipulative and selfish tendency," he accused, "I would have never invited you to live with me, and never suggested that we collaborate." "After all," he continued, "I am a welcome guest everywhere I go, and I have so many places I can live."

When he finished bragging about his

options, he even called me ungrateful and told me I had made him miss his boat by causing him to ignore so many grand invitations while he wasted time coddling a baby like me.

"I am most sought after and don't you ever forget that," my false ego told me. "Practically everyone consults with me and wants my association. But if you no longer desire my services, if you have no present assignment for me, then I will just leave here immediately." But then, with a long pause, he added, "Of course, I can stay around a little longer if you really want me to."

Now that he has spoken to me in this way, I have mixed feelings. Here is someone I've done everything with. We have so much history together, it is as if we are soul mates. Yet, in spite of the deep attachment between us, now he is ready to walk out of my life forever, taking all of his gaudy decorations.

When I thought about my false ego leaving me, I became furious. Then, moments later I felt devastated, as I thought of how he had viciously used me. "I want nothing whatsoever to do with you," I screamed at him. But now that he had packed up all of his belongings and was standing at the doorway, ready to exit, I realized how frightened I was of being alone.

"What will it be like to live without him," I thought. "He has been my steadiest companion. There's no part of my life that he hasn't touched. Should I just keep him around and use him only when it's necessary? Or should I find him a place close by so we can "hang out" together on special occasions, like maybe when guests come by, or when I need to impress others?"

Of course the problem was, if I kept him nearby, I had no guarantee I could control him because in the past his nature always prevailed above mine. His desperation for fame made him so much stronger and more clever than me, I could never resist his proposals. So what would make things different now?

I wanted to demand that he leave immediately, but the closer he got to leaving, the scarier his absence seemed. The very thought of living without my false ego was threatening. But in spite of my fear, I watched him pick up his belongings and leave, offering him no help whatsoever—not even waving goodbye.

As he left, I just sat back in my chair, feeling deserted, exploited and sad. But although my body was still and motionless, inside my mind was racing.

"What is the advantage of having so much knowledge," I asked myself, "if it simply leaves you in a lonely state of existence? What is the advantage of getting rid of unwanted things if there is no ultimate fulfillment?" Tears began to flow from my eyes as I pondered these mysteries. "It's so unfair," I thought, wiping my teardrops.

Suddenly I was taken aback. "Is it true what I am seeing?" I looked around me. With the tears gone, I now had a clear vision, and the entire sight was incredible. Everything in the house was transforming before my eyes.

When my false ego was here, he always told me that this was "our" property—something for our mutual enjoyment. But in that state of consciousness, all the books, furniture and art in our midst merely felt like a burden. But now, with my false ego gone, all the articles scattered throughout God's house took on a new vibrancy. In fact, each article looked almost alive, as if it were smiling and glowing with inner warmth.

All this affected me deeply and a calm sense of well-being came over me. In fact, before I knew it, even my senses followed suit and, as if stimulated by the transformed environment, they too participated in the celebration by giving me a rush of positive emotions.

Suddenly I could understand how dull I had previously been to give so much attention to my false ego and his imaginings. But now that he and I have parted company, there are so many wonderful things I can experience that I cannot describe my excitement.

42 The Beggar III

Meditation 4

The false ego brings on spiritual suicide

All *bona fide* religions have a goal that is obtainable through authentic mentorship. The mentor or spiritual guide is called by different names according to the tradition. In Islam the mentor is called Imam; in Sufism, Sheikh; Pi in Gnosticism, Hierophants in Christian Mysticism; Staretz in Eastern Christianity; in Hasidism, Zaddik; in Zen, Roshi and in Tibetan Buddhism, Lama.

In the Vedic tradition, the primary mentor is called the spiritual master or Guru. No one can make serious advancement in this tradition without the mercy of the Guru. One must fully understand that by the causeless mercy of God (Krishna), one gets a *bona fide* Guru, and by the mercy of Guru one gets Krishna. Developing God consciousness is synonymous with developing Guru consciousness.

Therefore, because I have become such a great Guru, and I am eager for all of my disciples to develop Krishna consciousness, I must tell them how to live solely to satisfy me. Surely this would please my Guru.

My Dear disciple, give up who you think you are and become a puppet for me. Whenever you are thinking of something, always consider: "is this how my spiritual master thinks, or how he would want me to be thinking at this moment?" When your answer is "yes, this is how Guru thinks or how he would want me to think," then you can know for sure that you are making spiritual advancement. But when you are in doubt or know that I would not be pleased, then know that you are committing spiritual suicide.

My dear disciple, give up who you think you are and become a puppet for me. When you hear something you must consider whether the sounds and discussions are the kind of things your Guru wants to hear. As you speak on various topics, you must ask yourself if your message would be pleasing to your Guru. When you have doubts about what you are hearing or speaking, or when you know it would definitely not please me, know that you are committing spiritual suicide.

My dear disciple, give up who you think

you are and become a puppet for me. When you observe various activities and scenes in your environment, ask yourself if what you are viewing is something your Guru would also want to see. Imagine me sitting next to you. If you feel or know I would not appreciate what you are viewing, know that you are committing spiritual suicide.

My dear disciple, give up who you think you are and become a puppet for me. As you interact in various environments, people will treat you in different ways. Sometimes, it will be confusing for you to process what your feelings should be. But as you are living for me you must think, "how would my Guru interpret each situation, or how would he want me to feel about each encounter?" If you feel or know that I would not be pleased by your interpretations or feelings, you should know, once again, that you are committing spiritual suicide.

My dear disciple, give up who you think you are and become a puppet for me. There are so many things that can distract you from your short and long-term goals. A disciple must remain very focused, and must use his or her time wisely. It is no longer only your time; it is Guru's and Krishna's time as well. One should constantly reflect on how they are using the Guru's time. If you are not time conscious, if you waste, misuse or abuse time, you should know that you are committing spiritual suicide.

My dear disciple, give up who you think you are and become a puppet for me. These days, people do not honor the various orders of life and rites of passage. Most of their actions are based on situational ethics and relativism. They do not understand the science of what is to be done or how it is to be carried out. Your actions should always be based on what my own responses would be in each situation. When you act on your own whim, know that you are committing spiritual suicide.

My dear disciple, give up who you think you are and, as I have constantly explained, become a puppet for me—your spiritual master. One of the most difficult areas in pursuing transcendence is to give up one's will in the service of Guru and Krishna (God). This means surrendering every aspect of one's being, including aspirations for Guru's service. This is the perfection of being a puppet for the guru and becoming a full instrument of empowerment. Today I want to explain how the disciple offers his will to his Guru.

As I sat down before many disciples in full readiness to again explain to them how they must offer me their will, I beheld a vision of my own Guru. He looked at me at first with anger, and then with sadness as he spoke to me. "Bhakti-tirtha, although the words you speak are correct, you are in no position to tell anyone how to offer their free will back to Krishna. You must demonstrate this with your very being. How will you teach them this pure science when your own thinking, feeling and willing are so impure? Have you fully become a puppet for me?"

Guru continued: "First, become fully surrendered to Guru and Krishna yourself; then your own example will convince those under your care to follow your lead."

"What a huge false ego you have in demanding from others what you yourself are lacking!" he continued. "Do you think you are a first class mentor? I have sent you disciples so you can prepare them properly for devotional service. But even more important, I have sent these disciples to teach you how to become a better disciple yourself!

"My request is that *you* give up who *you* think *you* are and that *you,* once and for all, stop committing spiritual suicide!"

Guru's words reverberated in my heart: "Do not delay in fulfilling this order—this may be the last time I can return to save you!"

"The Vedic scriptures explain that when the elderly, women, Brahmins, children and cows are protected and cared for, civilization will prosper."

Meditation 5

It's not enough to only listen

As a great leader, I am aware that one of the important qualities of a leader is to be an empathetic listener. Everyone feels a need to be heard, but it is not enough to only listen. Many people come to speak with me about all different types of problems. Being extremely merciful, I make time for everyone, and I am most expert in offering sound advice. I add such value to society, especially because I am very attentive to the elderly, women, Brahmins, children and cows.

The Vedic scriptures explain that when the

elderly, women, Brahmins, children and cows are protected and cared for, civilization will prosper. Conversely, when any of these innocents are not cared for, those who neglect them will experience shortened lives and great suffering. How fortunate the people are to have me as their spiritual guide.

The first recipient of my mercy today was an elderly gentleman. He was very weak and sickly. He walked in slowly, having trouble balancing himself. He stood up for quite some time waiting for one of my assistants to bring him a chair. But, as soon as he sat down, I knew just how to help him. I started telling him about how important the elderly people are because they can impart wisdom to others. I also consoled him by saying that he is not his body, but an eternal spiritual being. I am sure my hour of preaching gave him great solace. Maybe one of these days I will ask him to share some of his wisdom. But at least he has been fortunate enough to hear from me at this late stage of his life, before he crosses over.

Following the elderly man came a young lady seeking my mercy. I put on some nice music and lit fragrant incense to elevate the atmosphere to be sure that she could easily assimilate my sacred words. The woman graciously offered respect to me, and then began explaining how lonely she was. I interrupted her to explain that Krishna is in everyone's heart and that she should therefore never feel alone. "The Lord is never oblivious to our grief," I told her, "and the Lord's devotee is even more compassionate than He is," I enthusiastically consoled her. "But if ever you feel unbearably lonely, you can always visit me and partake of my nectarean words of flowing mercy."

Being so expert and experienced, all these healing instructions I gave her took only an hour for me to deliver. I had much more enlightenment to offer her, but I thought this would be enough to hold her until our next visit. Anyway, how fortunate she is to have a male advisor like me in her life to ingeniously stimulate her with sacred wisdom.

My next visitor was a learned brahmin. He sat down humbly on the floor in the lotus position and showed me several pieces of special writing from the Goswamis. He wanted to share a particular quote with me from these papers, but if I allowed such a digression, there would be little time left for me to give him my quality association. Steering the conversation to where it needed to be, I told him how wonderful he is and what an important asset to the community he is. I made special mention of the powerful classes he gives, his extensive knowledge and his constant referencing of the sastra.

All this I also accomplished in just an hour, but since a leader like me always has to be time-conscious, I dismissed the brahmin to make room for all the other people waiting to receive my mercy. "During his next visit," I thought, "I should surely ask him to share some scriptures with me. But, given all the demands on my calendar, and all the people who are eager for my association, I'm not sure when I'll be able to fit him in again. Well, at least I have given him my full attention this time around. I can't say when the Lord will shower my blessings on him again, but I guess that will all depend on his eagerness for it."

My next visitor was a beautiful little child. She began explaining to me that since coming into my zone, she has felt very neglected and unprotected. I immediately interrupted her to remind her that in our spiritual bodies we are all youthful, and that eternal youthfulness in Krishna's service is actually our inherent position. I explained how she, above all, should never feel overlooked or ill-treated because her situation as a child is enviable. "Look in the mirror. You are blessed with youth, my child. Don't you know that all adults are hankering to regain their eternal, youthful natures?" She began to whimper a bit as if bewildered, so to give her more solace, I explained: "If you're concerned about protection, little one, you can always think of me as your constant protector, and you always know where to find me. I am always seated right here in these comfortable quarters, ministering to the needs of the people."

Then, not wanting to be unfair to anyone else, I gave her a tissue to wipe her eyes as I dismissed her to see my next guest. As she left, I wondered where she was headed when she left me, and where she had come from. "Maybe on one of her future visits, I'll ask her—if there is time," I thought to myself. "Still, we must count the child among the fortunate. After all, she too has been the recipient of my direct attention and thoughtful consideration."

I was relieved to see that another adult was entering my office. He had an entire pad full of questions about the philosophy of Krishna consciousness. After the first of these questions, I interrupted him to explain all the things that new devotees are expected to know. Since he's an attentive listener, I'm sure just a few sessions of hearing from me will give him a strong basis in the science of bhakti. Maybe during one of his future visits, I'll let him share his list of questions, but I'm sure these will never match the quality of my own offerings to him. Besides, having already given him the mercy of my association, there's really no need to address any of his questions. But I'm sure he'll be fine now that he has interacted with a mature spiritual personality like myself.

The next person to enter the room was one of my dearest disciples. He is so advanced that even before offering me his respects, he started glorifying me and saying that I was a merciful expansion of my own Guru. I listened so well to this qualified disciple that I can repeat his words verbatim. "We can see this mercy manifest, Gurudeva, in your kind eagerness to help everyone." He then offered me prostrated obeisances and resumed my glorification, reciting prayer after prayer and commenting on my wonderful qualities.

This went on for almost two hours, and he

was so eloquent that there was no need for me to interrupt him. Unlike most of the needy and neophyte individuals who come to see me, this disciple is a very advanced soul who understands the essence of bhakti and just how fortunate he is to have me as his spiritual director. Knowing that he always has important things to share, I listened very well to this special disciple for the entire time that he spoke, and I entirely lost track of time.

Over an hour ago, I was supposed to visit the barn to speak with a cowherd boy and see how the cows are being cared for. I was so absorbed in my last meeting that I missed the appointment altogether, but I'm sure it's okay. As a selfless servant of humanity, I am always available to help so many people—especially the elderly, women, brahmins, children and cows.

Surely Guru and Krishna see how diligently I am working on their behalf. After all, I make myself fully available to every and anyone who comes to see me. The proof is how well I have trained up my best disciples. Just like the last one who visited me. He is so well trained that I did not even have to speak very much to him.

Seeing what good results my companionship has produced in him, I wish that I could give everyone who crosses my path the mercy of my extended guidance and association. But unfortunately I am only one person.

When will the day come that all my visitors will match that disciple's level of understanding? I expect to live a long life due to my compassionate nature and selfless desire to listen to everyone's concerns. Of course, natural born leaders like me know that it is not enough to only listen. Those of us who really want to benefit society have to be prepared to make the ultimate offering and sacrifice—we must be prepared to give out the mercy of our guidance and association.

For some reason, however, I am still experiencing illness and bodily suffering, despite my attentive care of the elderly, women, Brahmins, children and cows. Obviously, I must be prepared to give even more of my mercy.

"My dear spiritual master," I wrote in another letter, "One of the most difficult instructions you gave me was to be selfless."

Meditation 6

Think more of others
and less of yourself

My dear spiritual master, over the years in my service to you, one of the most difficult instructions you gave to me was for me to be selfless. Normally when I think of being self-less, anxiety flares up in my heart and mind. The thought naturally arouses emotions of fear, for I can't help feeling that this means giving up my entire identity—all my needs and aspirations. It sounds like you're instructing me to become a doormat for others' desires, and to become a non-entity.

When you instruct me this way, my false ego screams: "No way! That is total insanity!"

Thank you so much for showing me by your lifestyle that being selfless does not mean giving up my identity, but reclaiming my pure and royal identity. It does not mean I must give up my needs, but I must replace my desires with the actual, pure needs that are eternally attached to my soul. Can you speak some words that will further enlighten me about the need for selflessness?

My spiritual master spoke: "Of course, my son. Selflessness is the ingredient most lacking in today's world, because people misunderstand the purpose and principle behind this wonderful science. Genuine selflessness is not about thinking less of yourself, it's thinking of yourself less."

My mentor continued: "Selflessness does not mean to give up pursuing adventurous goals, but rather to attach ourselves to transcendental goals. Actual selflessness means we must genuinely access humility and submissiveness. This can be very scary, because we normally identify humility and submissiveness with low self-esteem.

"Low self-esteem can cause people to give up their identity and their ability to explore, create and achieve, while letting others control their thoughts and actions. But this is never the result of genuine selflessness. Genuine selflessness is an empowering process that grants us more and more autonomy."

I pondered my master's words and then revealed more of my apprehensions: "My dear spiritual master, one of the most difficult instructions you've given me is to be selfless. I want to obey this order, but doesn't being self-less mean that I will eventually grow bored and lazy, for I will always be absorbed in helping to serve and facilitate others? Doesn't being self-less mean I will never experience satisfaction?

"There are so many people suffering in impoverishment. Wars are going on every-where. People are dying from so many diseases. There is abuse of children, women, natural resources, the elderly and even the mentally ill. People on this crazy planet abuse their spouses and take drugs. So many "-isms" pervade every corner of the earth, and the planet is dying from toxicity. Where we don't find poverty and tribalism, we find religious fanaticism and mental illness.

"These days, everyone is suffering: The atheists, the materialists and the spiritualists. Being selfless means to always be eagerly occupied in trying to assist in the healing process of the planet, its leaders, its institutions and its people. By your mercy my dear spiritual guide, I can now understand that genuine self-lessness is not about thinking less of myself, it's thinking of myself less."

This time I decided to write my mentor. "My dear spiritual master," I wrote, "one of the most difficult instructions you gave me was to be selfless. I normally look at all kinds of sights for my enjoyment. My ears are very active in trying to hear something for their enjoyment. And my nose, mouth and stomach never take a vacation from searching for more material enjoyment. My genitals also never retire from anticipating illicit activity.

"I can understand that if I were truly self-less, none of these pulls from my senses would be a problem, for I would not allow my mind to give into the harassments of the environment, or into my egocentric desires.

"By your mercy my dear spiritual guide, I can now understand that genuine selflessness is not about thinking less of myself, it's thinking of myself less."

"My dear spiritual master," I wrote in another letter, "one of the most difficult instructions you gave me was to be selfless. I am so covered with jealousy and envy. But if I were truly selfless I would be happy to see others excel and achieve. My real happiness would not be in my own accomplishments but in the success of others.

"I would feel their sadness, pain and failures, as well as their happiness, joy and success. Until this is a spontaneous and natural reaction, I know that I am far from being selfless. I am still absorbed in so many fears coming from all of my senses, mind and even intelligence. If I want to become truly selfless, I realize that I must see, smell, hear, taste, speak, feel and do only those things that I know would be pleasing to you.

"Actually, anytime I think that I am the enjoyer, I am destined to experience fears and agitations. And every time I experience such disturbances, I must see it as another sign of selfishness.

"By your mercy my dear spiritual guide, I

can better understand that genuine selflessness is not about thinking less of myself, it's thinking of myself less."

I wrote letters for months... "My dear spiritual master, one of the most difficult instructions you gave me was to become selfless. If I took this seriously I would take care of all the things and people under my jurisdiction, and I would treat all of my possessions with utmost care. I would never be incompetent, impersonal, insensitive or neglectful, for I would realize that everything belongs to God and must be offered back to Him in such a way that the real Owner would be pleased. All that we consider ours has come to us by Krishna's mercy and will one day be taken away, therefore we are only caretakers.

"The fact that I am often incompetent, impersonal, insensitive and neglectful confirms that I am selfish and overly possessive. I am not properly recognizing who the real Owner is or how I should treat His possessions. By your mercy my dear spiritual guide, I can further understand that genuine selflessness is not about thinking less of myself, it's thinking of myself less."

My mentor encouraged me to write more on this theme, saying I had not yet explored it deeply enough. "My dear spiritual master, one of the most difficult instructions you gave me was to be selfless. If I had more gratitude, and more importantly if I did not minimize and doubt your and Krishna's mercy, I would surely be a more loving and selfless servant!

"You have been so kind to help me understand how I minimize your mercy. My selfish attachments and perceptions have caused me to hold onto low self-esteem or pride, pursuits of sense gratification, fears and jealousy, enviousness, incompetence, impersonalism, insensitivity, neglectfulness, doubts and lack of gratitude.

"By your mercy, I now clearly understand that genuine selflessness is not about thinking less of myself, it's thinking of myself less. But I admit that I am perplexed. Why has this been such a difficult instruction for me to follow?"

My spiritual master replied, "Yes my beloved, not only will this continue to be a difficult instruction to honor, but it will be impossible for you to fully honor as long as you are convinced that you can do it on your own strength. But, as you more genuinely accept my grace and mercy, you will receive even more empowerment to rise above these remaining blocks."

"Beloved," my mentor continued, "it is actually far simpler than you think. Simply continue thinking of yourself less and your whole existence will become more infused with the glorious, sublime mercy of our worshipable Lord and His Divine Consort."

Meditation 7

Being selfless, humble and brave

Many people die very young. Others live out their normal life expectancy, and others can live beyond the average life expectancy. In some parts of the world, the average age a person can expect to live is only forty-six years, due to war and diseases. In many of the countries in Europe and America, the average life span is around seventy-five years.

I am over fifty years old at the time of this writing, so, if I am average, I can expect to live around twenty-five more years. I may of course live for less time or perhaps longer, but since I must inevitably leave this body, let me reflect

"*I have already wasted so many of my years by being ungrateful and lamenting... I must become truly selfless, humble and brave.*"

on all the failures, challenges, and accomplishments I've made in my life with reference to the ultimate goal.

I've prayed and cried out for help from my various guides for clarity about my status. These guides have inspired me to see that going more deeply inward and reflecting is the first step I must take. As I look back, it seems there was never a time that I was without powerful mentors, but in spite of the great legacy they wanted to give me, I was never sufficiently selfless, humble or brave.

My mentors were extremely tolerant and valuable, though I rarely appreciated their virtuous qualities, and was often very demanding and ungrateful. Because of my immaturity, I frequently doubted and challenged them. I even secretly compared them with each other, or compared myself to them. Despite my admiration for them, I often only accepted the advice I wanted to hear.

My worst crime was in expertly taking credit for those things that had clearly come to me only because of their mercy. Worse than that, however, I never fully shared with any of them how much I appreciated their wonderful guidance because I was never sufficiently selfless, humble or brave.

For as long as I can remember, I have been a seeker of knowledge and truth. Even today, I am constantly reading to understand things that I see. Now, by the grace of so many masters' books, I know almost everything I ever wanted to know; but in truth I have forgotten most of this knowledge, if I ever actually understood it in the first place. I have read and heard so much, but understood so little. I have tried to possess knowledge and truth through my mind and intelligence, but because I am never sufficiently selfless, humble or brave, I have mainly acquired information and data, while only superficially connecting with truth, wisdom and knowledge.

Being a very restless person, I am always eager to travel far and wide. I have been to every continent and visited most countries. I have met thousands of wonderful people at the different classes, seminars and workshops I've given. Others have heard me lead kirtan or perform at festival functions. Even though my disciples, god-brothers and god-sisters are so kind and accommodating to me, I usually take them for granted because I am never sufficiently selfless, humble or brave.

I have always loved culture and entertainment. On the path of Bhakti-yoga there are always feasts, festivals, art and culture that involves dancing, singing and theatrical performances. Between those and the many rites of passage, almost every day in ISKCON is a festival. Although I bring my body to attend many of these events, often I am not really fully present. Sometimes I wonder why this is the case, but the answer is very obvious: I do not fully absorb myself in the culture of Bhakti because I am not sufficiently selfless, humble or brave.

Being a microcosm of the global community, family is another extremely important social element. I have a large biological family and a sizable spiritual family. Both of my families love me dearly and often inconvenience themselves on my behalf. Many of them even sacrifice their time and money to see me, but how do I reciprocate with them? Often I almost totally ignore them, or just serve them in a utilitarian way. Perhaps if I were more selfless, humble and brave, I could find time to serve them more sincerely.

Since I absolutely adore being praised, anyone who flatters me can get almost anything they want from me. In addition to praise, I appreciate respect and congratulations. But when I am ignored or criticized, I feel hurt, insulted and even angry. Sometimes I hold grudges or lament these insults for months or years. Of course, anyone who praises me can have my lifelong friendship and well wishes, even if he does so with devious and duplicitous motives.

Blaming others is an art I have mastered so expertly that no matter what the situation is, I have a way to shift the blame from myself. Like a tennis pro, I can deflect any blame as soon as a criticism hovers in my vicinity. I always see others at fault, and never see my own contribution because I lack sufficient selflessness, bravery and humility.

Here I am, close to death, yet I am forced to wonder how I can still be so superficial. I often have opportunities to help someone preach or stand up for righteousness, truth and integrity. I, however, always wait for another person to jump in and take the reigns. While waiting, I rationalize that I am too busy to help and have more important activities to pursue. I have done this so much that I have forgotten to feel guilty for my neglect and convinced myself that my lack of acting is noble rather than lazy cowardice. If I were not so proud and selfish, surely I could access more bravery.

Lord Krishna has said that He personally rewards each person as they surrender. Surrender does not mean that we think less of ourselves, but rather that we think of ourselves less. By thinking of ourselves less and of others more, we can become truly selfless.

First class devotees are so appreciative of others and are so eager to serve that they have very little time to worry about themselves. Krishna, noticing such a devotee, takes away all his or her personal problems so he or she can continue to serve others nicely. Krishna also carries to such devotees what they lack and maintains what they have acquired.

Being humble is another aspect of surrender. To be humble means to allow room for Radha and Krishna's love, sweetness and greatness to come through. Being humble means to recognize the importance of the great legacy left by the Vaishnava acaryas. Being humble means to worship and scrutinize the scriptures. Being humble means to rejoice when others are successful and feel their pain when they suffer setbacks.

Bravery is one of the most important

aspects of surrender. One cannot be transcendentally brave without first being selfless and humble. Unless one is truly selfless and humble, one will not value others sufficiently and will therefore mainly act for his or her own so-called welfare. Where there is proper selflessness and humility, a devotee will eagerly become the servant of others. A selfless, humble devotee is so brave that if necessary, he or she will stand alone to defend truth and integrity, despite being in the minority.

The brave devotee is determined to represent the acaryas and give only his or her best offerings to them. A brave devotee is the finest spiritual warrior because he fights on the subtle battlefield of consciousness with weapons of compassion, truth and love. A brave devotee monitors his actions and is guided by guru, sadhu and sastra. Thus, he or she proceeds with great confidence and competence.

It is obvious that I will die soon, and when I look at my present status, I realize I am lacking in three of the most important Vaishnava qualities. I am not sufficiently humble, selfless or brave, and there is hardly sufficient time to transform my character. I have already wasted so many of my years being ungrateful and lamenting. My obstacles are very clear to me now. I must become truly selfless, humble and brave. But even knowing what I must develop and work on doesn't diminish the task, for my false ego also knows this and it has designed many means to destroy my attempts.

How will I be able to fully help myself surrender when I am my own greatest enemy? I have only a little time left to become selfless, humble and brave, but my false ego laughs and accuses: "It's already too late, you failure. Just look at how many times you've tried and failed before."

If only I can muster the bravery, I will prove my false ego wrong. Dear Sri Sri Radha Damodara, because You are my only hope, I beg You to give me sufficient selflessness, bravery and humility before it really is too late!

Meditation 8

Illness as a special gift from God

Illness can be one of the most amazing gifts from God. When our bodies break down, we get an extraordinary opportunity to pursue higher consciousness. When we are in good health, the tendency is to take everything for granted. Personally, when I am in good health, I am mostly concerned with eating, sleeping, mating and defending. When my body is diseased, however, I have little desire to eat. At best, I can try to remember how wonderful it was to enjoy a tasty meal, but even still, I have little incentive to try to fulfill my appetite because I know that eating will wreck my health even more.

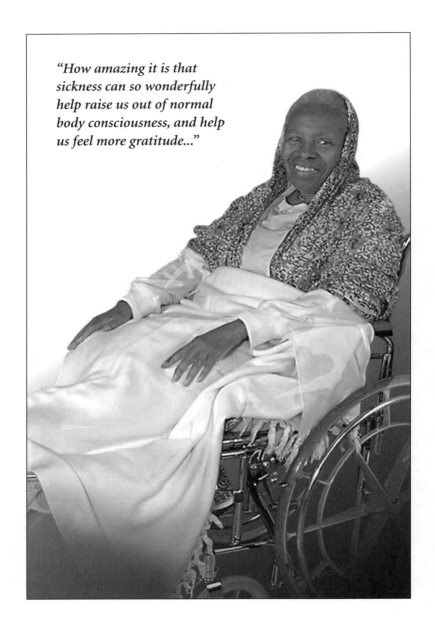

"How amazing it is that sickness can so wonderfully help raise us out of normal body consciousness, and help us feel more gratitude..."

Sometimes when sickness overcomes me, I think of sleeping and realize how important it is to be able to rest peacefully during the night. Unfortunately, when I am sick insomnia sometimes plagues me and I never feel fully refreshed.

As for mating and defending, in a state of wellness I sometimes contemplate the adventures of battle and sex life. On the other hand, when I am sick, even thinking about these acts becomes bothersome, and I have no energy or interest in either of these things. Thus, sickness and all of its sufferings can actually help us raise ourselves out of the bodily concept, and help us center ourselves on God.

Sickness can be one of the most amazing gifts from God. When we become ill, we get an extraordinary opportunity to pursue higher consciousness. I am often full of pride and am desperately seeking prestige. When I'm sick, however, I naturally become humbled and I become totally disinterested in distinction.

Being in a material body means that we are eager to enjoy sense gratification and other imaginings of the false ego. Sickness can help raise us out of the bodily conception by putting us deeply into bodily suffering. Thus, sickness can be one of the greatest boons from God.

I am often a poor manager of time, and I procrastinate beginning projects that should be started with concentrated vigor. I do this because I falsely believe that I can do so many things in the future. Thus, I often forget the important things that I have put off doing for some other occasion, and sometimes even put secondary things before these primary requirements.

When I am ill however, all this becomes crystallized. In fact, it becomes very easy for me to prioritize my affairs during illness, because I immediately get a clear vision of what is important and what is trivial or unessential.

When I am ill, I am acutely aware of sensations. Every second of each moment is registered in my consciousness. Each moment that my pain continues seems like an eternity. But, whenever there is just some slight relief of my pain and discomfort, I feel a wonderful sense of gratitude and I am utterly appreciative.

It is unfortunate that when I am well, I am so oblivious to the passage of time and my egotistic entanglements make me insensitive to reality.

How amazing it is that sickness can help raise us out of normal body consciousness, and can help us feel more gratitude for the gifts we usually take for granted.

Sickness can be one of the most amazing gifts from God. When we are ill, we get a great opportunity to pursue higher consciousness. When we are suffering, the worst and best parts of our nature come out. Suffering due to illness makes people doubt God's mercy and love. Chronic illness and pain can even cause intense anger and depression.

A diseased person's pain can be so severe that he will contemplate suicide and perhaps feel that he can no longer stand to be in his body. Persons in this condition, who have only excruciating pain to look forward to, begin to sympathize with others who have serious physical ailments and also suffer from chronic pain. Their own chronic pain can be such a wonderful opportunity to look deeper at the nature of the human condition, and the duality of the material world.

When I suffer, I feel even greater compassion for those who experience ongoing physical challenges. Suffering due to illness has allowed me to focus better on the limitations and illusory nature of material existence, and my experiences of illness have helped me to be more appreciative of my wellness.

Suffering with disease has helped me to better realize that there is no complete security or happiness in the material world. How amazing it is that sickness has forced me to reflect on higher values, and helped to raise me out of normal bodily consciousness while sensitizing me to deeper concerns.

Sickness can be one of the most amazing gifts from God. When we are ill, we get an amazing opportunity to pursue higher consciousness. No one can make serious spiritual advancement without first becoming desperate, determined and focused. Thus, Krishna often gives special mercy to some of His servants by putting them into life-threatening situations.

When these servants of the Lord experience major difficulties, it gives them a chance to cry out more intensely for mercy, clarity, growth and security. This intensely speeds up their spiritual acceleration, and allows them to cut through numerous layers of the false ego.

I can understand, Dear Lord, that you have blessed me so much by giving me some tangible experience of illness and helping me transcend my bodily consciousness. Because I am now submerged in bodily suffering, I can better perceive the unlimited tricks of my false ego. I can even understand the nature of my stagnations much better. I beg you Dear Lord, even if it means increasing my bodily discomfort, please do whatever is necessary to help me become a better servant of You and Your servants.

After all, Dear Lord, my desire is to transcend duality and all of its permutations. Knowing this desire of mine, surely whatever You subject me to will assist me in this effort.

Thank you Dear Lord, for allowing me to taste the mercy of illness. Sickness has helped me to rise out of normal bodily consciousness and has even heightened my compassion for others. Now, by Your grace, I can become more detached from all dualities, and I can more quickly walk away from the illusions of my false ego. Thank you, Dear Lord, for this disguised blessing of affliction, and thank You for letting me appreciate its special nature.

Meditation 9

Culture of rage

When my soul appeared before me this morning, I was more eager than usual to reveal my mind to him. I shouted, "I hate you! I hate this world and I hate everything connected with it! Everything about this life is miserable and absurd. I'm mad at you, at everybody and at everything in this dimension!"

My soul said nothing in return. Considering this an invitation to vent, I continued in my tirade.

"Behaving differently from the masses has been a waste of time. Even trying to think differently than the masses is a useless expenditure of energy. Once I return to living as they do, life will be normal for me again."

My soul decided to give me a revelation: "Do you really think you can get solace from returning to the prevailing mentality? Perhaps you should reflect more deeply on the genuine antidote to your suffering."

I wanted to scream some more, but instead I looked around me. In every direction I turned I was astounded to see one form of rage or another. On the roadways there is road rage. In the sky, there is airplane rage. Underground there is subway rage. In the malls there is shoppers rage, in the boardrooms there is executive rage. In the clinics there is hospital rage. At the universities, high schools and middle schools, there is students' rage. Will there one day be nursery school and day care rage? In the theaters there is actors' rage. Even at the polls and the sports arenas, there is voter's rage and fan rage.

There is practically no area of society that is not dominated by rage. I realized that I have joined a culture of anxiety, frustration and gloom. Still, I tried to defend my previous argument.

"Rage may be dominant and it has its consequences, but I am amazed at how foolishly optimistic it was of me to try to be loving and compassionate, while everyone and everything around me simply ignores or attacks me. When I join with society's winners, I will no longer be ignored and attacked. Rather, I shall have the joy and adventure of initiating my own attacks. But first, let me share with you my realizations about the reasons for rage.

"Birth itself is hell. A mother carries a baby for nine months. She gets fat, experiences sickness, has unusual cravings and suffers in the operation room delivering the baby. The baby also has its traumas.

"While in the womb, the embryo is attacked by worms, germs and bacteria, and it experiences stinging pains from what the mother eats, as well as many of her movements. Even when the mother is calm and still, the baby is packed up inside a sack in her womb in the most uncomfortable position.

"After so much torture, the baby is finally forced out of his mother's womb by her muscle spasms and by assisting medical attendants. To further assist the delivery process, the mother is sometimes told to feel rage as she pushes the baby out of her womb. And into what is she expelling this helpless infant whom she loves so very much? Into a world as cruel and hard as stone!

"Later, this child will harass his own mother with never-ending needs—to be fed, changed, comforted from fear, and protected from the cold. As much as the mother loves him, she cannot possibly tend to his every need, and so the child must wait until his mother can minister to him. In this waiting period, the child develops rage.

"It seems totally imbalanced. For one act of sex enjoyment, the mother has a huge medical expense. She may deliver a deformed baby or have unbearable medical complications due to problems with delivery. Either she or the baby may die in this arduous process, and in either case, the father will experience sadness and rage.

"For that one act of sexual pleasure—the anticipation of which was far better than the experience—a mother will have to deal with the father of her child for the rest of her natural life, or at least until their child reaches adulthood. Likewise, the father of this child, whether he wants to or not will have to financially support the child until he or she is an adult. Although he may hardly like or love the child or its mother, he will also have to relate to them for the rest of his natural life, or at least until their child is an adult. It all seems so imbalanced.

"Sometimes, during pregnancy and post pregnancy, a woman will experience rage at the man who impregnated her. Later, that rage may be transferred to the child or to both the child and father for any number of reasons. Similarly, the child's father will experience rage every time he thinks of how enslaving his role of supporting the family is.

"Ironically, even in best case scenarios where both parents offer their best loving care to their children, the children may develop rage toward their parents, especially during adolescence.

"Have you heard enough about the sources of rage, and why I and others have justifications for being so angry?" I asked my soul. "Or would you like to hear more about the culture of anxiety, frustration and gloom?"

My soul said nothing, so I took this as an invitation to vent more of my frustration.

"After he experiences the hardships of babyhood, the child finally goes to school. Although he has been carefully taught by his mother and father the principles of courtesy and kindness, he will be introduced to a new set of rules—where cutthroat competition is the game plan.

"At school, an observant child will notice that although no one admits it out loud, everyone is trying to outperform everyone else. Especially if that child is a girl, to survive, she will have to be taught to not fully trust anyone. Otherwise she may be sexually abused, perhaps even by her own father, uncle, grandfather, brother or priest."

My soul still patiently listened. "The girl who is molested will have to deal with her own sadness, anxiety and rage for the rest of her life. If a boy is similarly abused, when he seeks solace for his sadness, anxiety and rage, he'll either be laughed at and accused of being a sissy, or he will suppress his pain because he's been trained since birth to not show his emotions, and set himself up for many stress-related diseases of the body and mind.

"Are you convinced yet?" I asked my soul. "This is only the beginning, for as children grow up, they begin to see how the entire society is full of rage and hypocrisy. They will see how everything that pretends to offer them

shelter is just another trap for their exploitation."

"The children of this world quickly learn
that society teems with child abuse, spouse
abuse, sibling abuse, elderly abuse, ecological
abuse, drug abuse and more. They learn the
entire world is populated with angry people,
and that most of them are constantly abusing
one another and all the resources that are
available. These angry abusers will pretend to
be civilized, but on closer inspection, children
will see that all this is merely a show.

"Our once innocent children will wonder
why everyone pretends and covers-up their
penchant for violence, as if they don't enjoy it.
But the cover-up is very thin. All the games
and television shows available on the public
market—in fact everything that is popular in
the world centers itself on violence, abuse and
rage."

"Any child can see that most toys, television shows and movies are nothing less than
rage factories. Nations, tribes and ethnic
groups go to war and display so much rage that
they even engage in plots of ethnic cleansing
and invent means for nuclear, biological and
chemical warfare.

"When the children learn how adults are so
violent to animals, how they spend all day in
hostile work environments, and how they have
so many violent forms of sports and recreation,
they aren't surprised that the citizens are
enraged. But even if they were surprised, children who take social studies in school will

discover that religious orders, political parties and other organizations are founded on aggressive agendas. Those children, who used to wonder why adults were so tense and irritable, finally realize that anxiety, frustration and gloom are natural and inevitable byproducts of their lifestyle."

My soul said nothing to appease me, so I continued. "I feel even more rage when I think of the millions of animals that are killed yearly. They're killed in experiments, they're killed for foodstuff and sometimes just for peoples' sick forms of entertainment. On top of that, millions of people throughout the world are starving, have no proper drinking water, have no means of earning and no means for obtaining healthcare. Young children are often forced into prostitution or forced to fight as child soldiers just to earn a plate of food."

My rage intensified as I contemplated the circumstances.

"On top of that," I shouted, "some people commit all of these crimes in the Name of God!" This last scream seemed to deplete all my energy, and now I began to just cry.

"I feel more anxiety, frustration and gloom when I think of how from birth until the end of life, our situations produce nothing but anxiety and rage. People rarely even get to have dignified deaths. Their deaths are surrounded by so much pain and despair that not only their bodies, but their minds often break down under the pressure. If that isn't enough, once someone finally dies, his or her relatives usually argue and fight over whatever money and assets the deceased has left behind.

"Sometimes family members become life-long enemies due to conflicts surrounding the death of a loved one. Thus, from the cradle to the grave, there is so much rage festering in peoples' hearts! People like me who try to deny this reality are simply foolish and out of touch!

"You, my soul, have preached to me that it is all about love, selflessness and compassion, but I beg to differ! Actually, it is all about anxiety, frustration, and gloom. Above all of this is simply RAGE!"

I fell to my knees waiting for a rebuttal. I cringed a bit and slumped my shoulders, expecting astringent words. But instead of being angry with me about my rage, my soul spoke incredibly loving words:

"My darling counterpart," he said to me. "You are correct. Entities on this planet have an extremely difficult existence. Although they seek pleasure, they instead get anxiety and frustration. Everywhere you look, people are disappointing, attacking and abusing each other. So many people have big hopes and plans, but in the end they get frustration and rage.

"It would seem that things are unfair, but in reality it is only that peoples' false egos are so strong that they cannot see or understand how hellish their predicaments are. Your own rage, however, is not as ordinary as it appears. Your own rage is a sign of your disgust with the many illusions. It is a sign of the genuine love and pity that you have for the suffering of others. So never think of giving up your efforts to uplift the collective consciousness. Never accept the culture of anxiety, frustration and gloom, because, as you already know, that culture only produces more rage!

"But there is an alternative to this rage, and this is something you are also acquainted with. You must continue filling every corner of the world with the only antidote for rage—love, selflessness and compassion. If you continue doing this, you will eventually see a difference; if not in the world around you, then surely in your own mind.

"Beloved, I beg you to not give up dispensing your love with desperation. When the pressures get too intense, feel free to direct your rage at me. This way, there will be no negative consequence, for I know that your rage is no more than your love in a bewildered state."

I stumbled to the nearest mirror and looked deep into my own eyes, trying to see my soul. Although seeing him was impossible, I could hear his words very clearly. "If you direct your rage at me, I will accept it and will return it back to you as love. In this way, I will help to stabilize you as you make your last trek back to our full integration as one, in the service of the Divine Couple. I know in moments of rage and false ego you doubt that this is possible, but know that you are dearly loved, and that our final reintegration is imminent."

Meditation 10

The lover who comforts me

In my travels around the planet, the main things I see pervading the global community are pain, poverty, corruption, racism, violence, tribalism, death and disease. Although many people hide from these overwhelming realities, I know them to be true, yet I am completely undisturbed. You see, when I take shelter of the Lover who comforts me, these world catastrophes are no longer disturbing.

In times to come there will be increasing quarrels amongst religionists. Religious authorities with different outlooks will bicker, and many of their followers will lose faith in God altogether. As these authorities debate theology, many of their followers will let the pettiness, hypocrisy and immaturity of these so-called spiritual leaders disturb them to the point of agnosticism. Even scripture itself will seem to baffle people as they focus more on the contradictory nature of certain texts. But because I always take shelter of the Lover who comforts me, no degree of contradictions can disturb me.

Many stalwart leaders have deviated from the royal spiritual path, causing extreme pain and confusion to their students. These deviations have been a major embarrassment to the mission of the great teachers. When leaders become abusive of their flock, it shakes the very foundation of their congregations, undermines their institutions and makes many people question if God really cares. But, when I take shelter of the Lover who comforts me, none of these deviations are a source of disturbance.

The current level of abuse toward women and children across the planet is mind-boggling. During times of war or poverty, it is these gentlest of God's children who suffer the most exploitation. When women and children are not protected, society experiences all kinds of inauspicious karmic reactions. Yet, in these times, throughout all the institutions that comprise our government, education and commerce systems, women and children are treated like disposable commodities. There is little I can do to fix this, but when I take shelter of the Lover who comforts me, I get ideas of how to help reduce these hardships, and I feel compelled to do my part.

When I consider the world situation, it's easy to get angry with others for the mistakes and shortcomings they have contributed to the problem. Even worse, it's easy for me to become angry with myself for my own short-comings. When I study myself I see an avalanche of weaknesses, for I am below stan-dard in every department of life.

When I think of the facilities I have been given, and the wonderful opportunities that have always come my way, I become even more angered by my own incompetence. Sometimes I wonder to myself: "What is the use of my having ever been born?" But, when I take shelter of the Lover who comforts me, I realize that being angry with myself and others won't solve anything, because both anger and depression are reactive and counterproduc-tive.

In spite of this realization, quite often depression just suddenly overcomes me. Sometimes, depression even rides my back for days on end, like a wild cowboy prodding and kicking me whenever he chooses. Never satis-fied, my depression demands more and more attention from me and others, until the burden is almost unbearable. It's very hard to be joyful when pressed down by such depression, but sometimes it is a daily reality that makes it difficult to be creative and enthusiastic. Sometimes the struggle to overcome my sadness saps all of the energy I possess.

But when I take shelter of the Lover who comforts me, I realize that an obstacle is only something we see when we take our eyes off the goal. The fact is, depression need not be a choice that I opt for, and all the problems of this planet need not be problems that I personally own.

Still I have one enemy even greater than my depression that often totally dominates and dismantles me. That enemy is my all-devouring lust, which often directs my perceptions and activities throughout the day and night. During most of my waking hours, I see all things through a window of lust; in fact lust is what energizes my entire consciousness.

It is lust that stimulates me in all my thinking, willing and feeling, and it is lust that causes me to become attached to mundane concerns and achievements. It is lust that makes me angry when I am dissatisfied, and lust that causes most of my self-delusions. Lust has brought me again and again to this material world, and I am often completely unable to resist it. But, fortunately, when I take shelter of the Lover who comforts me, I am empowered to transform my lust into love.

Seeing my effort to understand, suddenly the Lover who comforts me spoke aloud. "You are correct; lust is your eternal enemy, but at the root of this lust is your false ego, which has caused you to embrace all of your confusion and illusion."

I was baffled to hear His voice. Generally, His way was to comfort me silently for very rarely did His remedies require language. But today He was choosing to accelerate my realization and growth.

"It is your false ego that causes you to develop all of your unhealthy perceptions and attachments. It is your false ego that prevents you from transforming your lust into love. In fact, beloved, it is even your false ego that invites depression to ruthlessly ride your back.

"As I have tried to tell you many times, E.G.O. means Edging God Out. Without God in the picture, you will never see things as they are. But, the good news is, now that you have let Me back in, soon all of your doubts and interferences will cease.

"How fortunate are you and all the entities who have a Lover that guides and comforts you, because although that grace originates in Me, the conduit for that grace is your spiritual master, and he is readily present and available. Actually, it is by the mercy of a bona fide spiritual master that one can magnify the voice of God!

"Because you have taken shelter of such a spiritual master, be assured that no personal or worldly problem will ever overwhelm you. In fact, nothing whatsoever can harm you. Nothing except for one thing... and that is the false ego that creates your disbelief."

"The crying of
Mother Mary has
been understood as
an expression of her sadness
owing to the sinful nature
of humanity."

Meditation 11

Cry with the Lord

Seeing or hearing about the Supreme Lord or His Deity cry is a very astounding experience. How can we understand this?

Early in the morning, as I rendered personal service to my Lord in His Deity form, I saw that His eyes were wet and tearing.

Many people have heard of or even witnessed the statues of the Blessed Virgin Mary crying and others have observed Jesus crying on the cross. The crying of Mother Mary has been understood as an expression of her love and compassion for all of God's creatures, and her sadness over the sinful nature of humanity. But how do we know that these stories are not just fables or exaggerations to inspire a doubtful population? This doubt often plagued my mind until I personally witnessed the crying of my Deity.

For sure, in whatever age it occurs, a statue crying is quite an astounding sight. How can we understand such a phenomenon?

The ancient Vedic scriptures describe the Supreme Person, Lord Sri Krishna, shedding humanlike tears. Upon seeing Grandfather Bhisma on the verge of death during the battle of Kuruksetra, Lord Krishna began consoling him with tears filling His eyes.

To appease the ailing hearts of all concerned, Krishna brought King Yudhisthira to Bhisma's outdoor deathbed so that Yudhisthira could hear Bhisma's instructions on ruling a kingdom righteously.

Even though the great warrior was wounded and dying, he gloriously carried out Lord Krishna's order with deep love and affection. Then, in the deepest of mutual meditations, Bhisma left the world thinking of the Supreme Lord as the Supreme Lord thought of him.

Seeing or hearing about the Supreme Lord cry is a very astounding experience. How can we understand this?

Sudama Vipra was a very poor brahmana who had associated with Krishna as a child. As schoolmates in the gurukula, the two boys learned and played together daily, but providence took the boys in different directions.

Sudama Vipra later married a chaste wife, but always remained extremely poor. Although learned in the sixty-four subjects of Vedic arts and knowledge, Sudama barely subsisted on the meager alms and income begged mainly by his wife. It was a number of years before Sudama and Krishna were reunited in Dwaraka, and by this point Sudama had become dangerously thin and malnourished. This is when Sudama's wife pleaded with him to journey into Dwaraka and beg some assistance from his rich friend, Lord Krishna, who was living in royal splendor. Although Sudama was reluctant to go, to placate his good wife, and because he was very enthused to see his beloved friend Krishna, Sudama walked all the way to Krishna's opulent palace.

When he entered the palace, Sudama was so overjoyed to see Krishna that he forgot his troubles. Since all of his desires were fulfilled by seeing Lord Krishna again, Sudama did not make any request of the Lord. He was even too embarrassed by the Lord's opulent surroundings to give Him the meager gift he had brought. But despite his bashfulness, Sudama was not only in utter bliss in Krishna's presence, but he also felt great guilt and unworthiness at receiving all the loving attention Krishna quickly showered on him.

The Lord was so attentive in His honoring of Sudama, that to an outside observer it might be difficult to tell which one was the Lord and which one was the devotee, for Krishna so devotedly worshiped Sudama that Sudama simply blushed and forgot all his worries, poverty and want.

As Krishna gently washed Sudama's feet in front of His magnificently attired queens, the Lord joked with Sudama about old times and worshiped him very lovingly. Although Sudama was embarrassed by all the attention he was getting from Krishna, he couldn't help relishing the Lord's presence.

When the all-knowing Lord realized how oblivious Sudama was to his own poverty, and how untinged and unmotivated his love for Krishna was, the Lord shed tears and further worshiped his unalloyed devotee.

Seeing or hearing about the Supreme Lord crying still remains an astounding phenomenon. How can we understand this? And who are these rare souls that can make the Supreme Lord cry?

The Pandavas were great devotees of Lord Sri Krishna who were exiled to the forest by their evil cousin. They were a royal family of princes previously living in luxurious opulence. Accustomed to very comfortable conditions, the Pandavas suffered immensely while in exile, despite the fact that they were so righteous and so very dear to the Supreme Lord.

For that entire period the Pandavas' lives were troubled with constant danger and discomfort. There were even several direct assaults on the Pandavas' lives, including an attempt to poison them and set their house ablaze while they were trapped inside.

Finally, at the battle of Kuruksetra, the

Pandavas were attacked by demons, and they had to take part in the world's greatest civil war, being called upon to engage in bloody battle against their very own kinsmen.

Lord Krishna was present on the earth at the time of that battle and aware of all the Pandavas' adversities. When the Lord reflected upon how his unalloyed devotees had to suffer due to their righteousness, His heart swelled and He shed huge tears, considering their long-standing grief.

Hearing about or seeing the Supreme Lord cry is a very astounding experience. How can we understand this?

The great yogi Kardama Muni underwent severe austerities to attract the mercy of the Lord. Kardama Muni fasted, prayed and sat meditating upon his worshipable Lord for thousands of years. When Lord Vishnu arrived to reciprocate with His devotee, the Lord was so overwhelmed with compassion that He flooded the area with His tears. These tears of the Lord came to be known as the holy lake *Bindu-sarovara*, and these waters are worshiped by holy sages and scholars even today.

The water of *Bindu-sarovara* is described as *sivamrita-jala*. *Siva* means curing, thus anyone who drinks the water of *Bindu-sarovara* is cured of all material diseases by the Lord's potency. Similarly, anyone who bathes in the waters of India's sacred Ganges River is relieved of all material diseases.

The Lord was so pleased with Kardama Muni and his exalted wife, Devahuti that He incarnated Himself in Devahuti's womb as their Son, Lord Kapiladeva. Indeed, the Lord's reciprocation with His devotees is nothing short of amazing!

Seeing or hearing about the Supreme Lord cry is very astounding. How can we understand this?

Srimati Radharani and Lord Sri Krishna are always sitting together enjoying each other's company. On one such occasion, a bumblebee mistook the golden lotus face of Srimati Radharani to be a lotus flower and began buzzing around Her exquisite visage, trying to enter that radiant flower. Radharani grew very upset with the bee for disturbing Them in this private moment. Witnessing the disturbance, Krishna's cowherd friend Madhumangala scared the bee away from the Divine Couple. Then, Madhumangala returned to the Divine Couple and proudly announced to Radha that the bee was gone.

In his hurry to relieve Radha's anxiety, Madhumangala used slightly garbled or broken Sanskrit and told Srimati Radharani "Ma-ha-su-hana (meaning the bumble bee) is gone." In Her distressed, half-crazed condition, however, Radha took Madhumangala's words to mean that Her beloved "Madhusudana" (Krishna) had gone.

Just the thought that Krishna had abandoned Her set Radha into a fit of lamentation. So drowned was Sri Radhika in an ocean of sorrow and separation that She began to cry torrents of tears for Her beloved, although Lord Krishna was present and seated right next to Her.

Because Her eyes were flooded with tears that impeded Her vision, Radharani couldn't even see Her Beloved Consort although he was just inches away. In that momentary gap of not seeing Him, Radharani's pain was so intense that She almost lost all life functions.

Seeing the intensity of Srimati Radharani's attachment to Him, Lord Krishna Himself then began to cry in ecstatic love. This crying continued for hours.

Radha's affection for Krishna and His for Her is always contagious and ever increasing. Thus, the tears shed by Their mutual crying formed a lake which is known as *Prema-sarovara*.

Seeing or hearing about the Supreme Lord cry is very astounding. How can we understand this?

In Krishna's special incarnation as Lord Chaitanya, He was constantly shedding tears of ecstasy and deep compassion. In the *Beda-kirtana* of congregational chanting and dancing, while the chanting occurred, there was a constant transference of ecstatic love, which featured such symptoms as perspiration, jubilation, trembling and fainting. As the Supreme Lord's direct incarnation in the loving mood of Srimati Radharani, Lord Chaitanya's love was irrepressible. The tears from the Lord's eyes came out with great force like water spraying from a syringe, and these tears moistened all those in His vicinity.

Seeing or hearing about the Supreme Lord cry is a very astounding experience. How can we understand this?

Because of the Lord's eagerness to assist His lost children in coming home, the pastimes He performs on the earthly plane and in all the other material universes often operate on multiple levels. For instance, the pastime of Lord Chaitanya's cleansing of the Gundica temple represents the need for the soul to cleanse his own dirty heart and mind.

As the Lord showed us, we should cleanse our subtle bodies very vigorously in our effort to know and serve the Lord, and in doing so, we should work in all humility without any sense of false prestige. Very appropriately, then, in this pastime, Lord Chaitanya allowed His outer body to become covered with dust and dirt in His cleansing of the holy temple. But despite being covered with the temple's dirt, He left that divine building spotless, and His own sacred body became even more transcendentally beautiful.

While cleansing the Gundica temple, the Lord used His tears as a liquid solvent to wipe the walls, floors and corners of the temple. Later, when the Lord would rest for a while and chant and dance with the devotees, again His tears would pour down like flood rains during the rainy season, and wash the bodies of all the devotees.

As Lord Chaitanya continued to dance before the Ratha Yatra cart, He trembled, perspired, roared and often rolled on the ground. Then more tears would manifest in a constant drip that flowed from the Lord's eyes. Sometimes these tears were so plentiful that the Lord had to check them so they would no longer obstruct His vision of Lord Jagannatha. Such was the ecstatic bliss experienced by Lord Chaitanya when He performed His pastimes of devotional reverie.

Seeing and hearing about the Supreme Lord crying can be a very astounding experience. How can we understand this?

There is a pastime in which Lord Chaitanya embraced His pure devotee, Ramananda Raya. Ramananda was a Governor and official of high stature in the secular world. Nevertheless, he was the purest of devotees, and when the Lord embraced Ramananda, both he and the Lord cried out in maddened ecstasy as they held each other.

Scholars of the day could not conceive why this great governing official was exuding so much emotion in the company of a renounced saint, or why the mendicant was so enthralled by the company of "a government man." But the Lord's pastimes are very bewildering and, no matter how clever or intellectually endowed one may be, non-devotees are never privy to the meaning of these pastimes.

The Lord's devotees not only behave eccentrically in the Lord's direct and indirect presence, but sometimes the requests they make of the Lord are quite extraordinary.

The exalted soul, Vasudeva Datta, for instance once requested of the Lord that he be allowed to suffer perpetually in a hellish condition and accept all the sinful reactions of the universe, so that all living entities could be liberated. "My Dear Lord, please transfer all the sinful karma of their lives upon me immediately," Vasudeva Datta begged the Lord.

When Lord Chaitanya heard Vasudeva's petition, His heart was completely melted. First, the Lord's lip and then other parts of His body began to tremble. Then, in a faltering voice, with tears pouring from His eyes, He explained to Vasudeva that he would not allow him to suffer such an agony, but that his request to spare the conditioned souls of the suffering they were due would be duly honored by the Lord because of His extreme affection for Vasudeva.

This is the great mystery of the Lord's crying. All the Lord's incarnations have complete and radiant love for Their devotees, and Their devotees are so completely enraptured with Them, that in their exchanges of love they are continually breaking records, and establishing new boundaries and precedents in the outpourings of their love.

The internal bliss and loving reciprocation the Lord gives His devotees cannot be described, and because the Lord's unalloyed devotees have boundless love for Him and know nothing other than the Lord, the Lord awards them with His personal association.

The Lord's pure devotees are totally selfless and full of compassion, and consequently they are totally devoid of any false ego. Thus, by their love for the Lord Himself and all of the Lord's parts and parcels, they have purchased the Lord entirely.

The Lord feels so grateful and indebted to His pure devotees for the intense love they display for Him, that He descends from His eternal abode, either in a Deity form or in His transcendental human-like form, and walks among us to display His captivating pastimes. In this way, the Lord receives and distributes large doses of divine love to His servants, so that they can forget the cares of this world and become fully re-established in their eternal occupation of rendering loving service to Him.

Now, by the Lord's grace I can understand that when the Lord comes before us and sheds tears, or when He causes His Deity form or a statue to do the same, He is doing this simply to invite us all to become His unalloyed devotees.

O, how I wish I could cry tears of separation from the Lord and not just tears of self-centered regret due to my material frustrations! But what can I do except for cry out in the hope that one day I will cry for, and eventually with, the Supreme Lord?

"*Liberated souls only want to eternally love and serve the Lord, but Krishna's only concern is our total welfare.*"

Meditation 12

Remove all barriers so that we can love each other completely

Conceptions of God are totally unlimited. The Supreme Personality is in fact so attractive that everyone throughout existence has discussed Him, and has had some theory about His existence or lack thereof. There are those, for instance, who say that God is just a figment of our imagination. Other theorists say that perhaps there was once a God who created the world, but that God has since vanished and is now irrelevant or even dead. Such persons have decided that God has no control over them or the events of this world, and so they postulate that even if God did exist, what would be His value?

Other persons, seeing the extent of evil and envy in the world, claim that a rather impotent and wishy-washy God does exist, but that He is not entirely good, and that He is definitely not omnipotent. There are also those who are uncertain about God's existence, but feel abandoned by Him and are therefore angry with Him. Resenting the suffering and hardship they've experienced, persons who feel this way even sometimes fantasize about killing God, if they ever have an opportunity to meet Him.

But these are just a few of the variant theories. In addition to God's "victims" and "abandoned," there are those who believe that God is nothing more than a Supreme Autocrat. That He is the last word and the Person who we must obey and must bow down to, or else be eternally damned.

Among the pervasive theories about God, there are even those who believe that God has always existed, but that He has never been any more than a soothing white light, a soothing sound or universal energy and mind. Persons who accept this concept of God actually believe that at some level of our being we all are God or are all gods, and that in time with some degree of effort we will recapture that status and become one with the Godhead or merge into Him.

Still, other speculators brazenly dare spiritualists to: "Show me God, in whatever form He or She exists in, then I will accept God's existence."

Dear Lord, I am praying to one day be

amongst those who can say, "If You are God, I don't care or want to know anything about You except how I can love and please You eternally. As for the details of Your personality, all I care to know about You is that You are the most perfect and wonderful friend, child, and lover, and that without serving You, I am incomplete. Therefore, please let everything else about You be unimportant to me so I can recognize that Your sublime Personality is the most satisfying and confidential expression of the Godhead."

But because I am not fully convinced, I read various scriptures to confirm this reality. Fortunately for me, the Torah discloses that Your servant Sarah related to You as mother and child. The Old Testament goes further to say that Your servant Moses also walked and spoke with You, friend-to-friend, and had face-to-face interactions.

Other scriptures corroborate this fact. Both the Holy Koran and the El Hadith speak of the Prophet Mohammed visiting the seventh Heaven and having friendly, face-to-face dealings with Allah. Prophet Mohammed even told his followers that God sometimes approaches him like a friend and puts His hand on his shoulders before giving him revelations.

The great Christian mystics Saint Francis of Assisi, Saint Teresa of Avila and Saint John of the Cross also spoke of having either personal friendships or amorous relations with the Lord.

Of course, unalloyed devotees of Krishna have no interest in relating to God in His aspect as the Supreme Controller. Nor do we want to experience the Lord as an All Pervading cosmic sound, light or energy. Krishna's devotees know that the Lord has millions of names that describe His inconceivable pastimes and potencies, but we do not want to know our Lord merely in some formal way. The Krishna devotee simply strives to know the Lord through pure loving exchanges that are devoid of stringent formalities. We want to taste love for our Lord through unmotivated, uninterrupted service, knowing full well that the thrill of performing that service will never grow stale or be anything less than super-extraordinary.

Because of the Lord's continual reciprocation with their service, Krishna's devotees know that no one can have a complete loving connection with another without ongoing interaction. Such devotees also know that an excess of awe and reverence can actually interfere with dynamic loving relationships with the Supreme. Though Krishna devotees know that the Lord is Almighty and Supreme, they gladly accept forgetfulness of these facts in order to experience the most confidential relationships with the Godhead.

Sometimes there is a great personality like a judge, king, or president of a country that all civilized persons show respectful etiquette to. But, the etiquette and formalities citizens direct toward these officials creates a barrier in the relationship between the parties, because both parties reveal only a part of themselves to the other.

At home alone with their grandchildren, such great, noble persons bounce these toddlers on their back and play "horsey," not minding that they are on their knees. Of course, to know that their granddaddy is an "important" person would only disturb the joy they derive from the games, so the grandchildren rarely reflect on the noble status of their parentage. Such a meditation would also dampen the flow of love from the grandfather if he were absorbed in his aristocratic status while playing with his grandchildren; the grandfather only wants to experience loving intimacy without any boundaries or formalities.

Once when the demigods were offering respectful prayers to Krishna, describing His glories and opulence, Arjuna stood beside Krishna with his hand on His shoulder in a mood of friendship, and nonchalantly brushed the dust from Krishna's peacock feather.

When the cowherd boys saw that Krishna had saved them from the forest fire by His mystic power, they began to think Krishna was a demigod. Absorbed in the meditation that Krishna was their dearmost friend, these boys also naturally assumed that since they are Krishna's peers, they too must be demigods.

When Krishna lifted Govardhana Hill, many of the residents of Vrndavana were fearful for Him, just as when He was in the wrestling match arranged by Kamsa. According to their rasa, various persons saw Krishna as their favorite playmate and best friend, their most charming and adorable child or their most irresistible and enchanting lover.

When Krishna danced on the hoods of the Kaliya snake, some of the residents of Vrndavana were again fearful, seeing Him in such a dangerous position. For them, Krishna was a favorite playmate, an adorable child or an enchanting lover, because they were experiencing the most confidential expression of the Godhead.

Nanda Maharaja and Mother Yasoda are fully captivated in loving sentiments for Krishna that make them experience Him as their most wonderful and charming son. Nanda and Yasoda think that Krishna is totally dependent on their loving care. In this way they give all their love to Krishna and He receives it fully.

For example, once when Mother Yasoda looked in baby Krishna's mouth, she was given the mystic perception to see all of creation. While looking in His mouth at all of wondrous creation, Yasoda momentarily realized Krishna's divinity. This completely disturbed her, and thus, in order to let her internal, pure affection again flow without reservation, Mother Yasoda immediately put aside the thought that Krishna might be the Supreme Lord.

Likewise, the gopis and gopas have no interest in knowing of Krishna's Supremacy. The gopis think only of Krishna's exquisite beauty, and feel drawn to Him as the most wonderful lover that ever existed. Similarly, the gopas think only of Krishna as their best friend and bravest heroic playmate. Above that, the gopas see Krishna as the supreme Source of their fun and amusement, thus they are always hankering for His company, and can't wait to play with Him and eat with Him daily.

Often, different gopas defeat Krishna in sporting, and yet they never apologize for this or regret it. The mood throughout Vrndavan is of total love without limitations, boundaries or formalities. There is not even a tinge of impersonalism or autocracy there, thus the residents experience the most confidential expression of the Godhead.

As I reflect on those who believe that there is no God or that God is dead or irrelevant, I cannot help but feel a bit sorry. And when I think of those who believe that God is no more than a bright light, or sound, the universal mind, or cosmic energy, I'm again saddened yet amused by their dilemma. Those who believe that they are or will one day become God especially bring a smile to my lips. By the Lord's grace, I am appreciating that God is many of these things, but also so much more.

For those who desire to be filled up with God, there is always the confidential aspect of the Godhead, where one can relate to the Lord as a friend, parent or lover. In all three cases, the Lord allows his pure associates to not only connect with Him in intimate ways, but He even allows such pure devotees to conquer and surpass Him!

This is all a part of the divine culture of bhakti, where one accepts and surrenders to the Supreme Lord fully, to later have the Lord remove all barriers, so that He can surrender Himself fully to His servant. This is the most confidential expression of the Godhead.

When I consider the immense joy and fulfillment atheists and speculators are denying themselves with all their doubts and delusional thinking, I simply grieve for their lamentable condition. More important, I now see the extreme importance of subduing and transcending my false ego. After all, it is the false ego alone that keeps me in the material world, trying to ignore or imitate the Supreme.

How amazing it is that the conditioned entities want to artificially deny our worshipable Lord, or just reduce Him to mere energy. It is even more amazing that these conditioned souls want to become God! Don't they know that our Lord is so kind and loving that He is ready to even allow us to outdo Him?

Liberated souls only want to eternally love and serve the Lord, but Krishna's only concern is our welfare. This is a fantastic competition that goes on and on eternally; a competition that our sweet Lord will always win.

The Lord wins to be the Loser, and loses to be the Winner—always engaging in whatever it takes to be completely controlled and captured by His unalloyed devotee. Krishna doesn't care whether we want to capture Him as a friend, a parent or as a conjugal lover. He is only concerned that we are prepared to give up all remaining traces of our false ego so that we can be fully enraptured by the love of our merciful Lord.

Never forget that Krishna's only interest in subduing you is that by so doing, the pure love for Him that you experience will conquer Him fully.

114 The Beggar III

Meditation 13

Devastated from exposing the illusion

We are constitutionally eternal beings, however, humanity relentlessly embraces temporary events and pleasures as if they are eternal. Every day, we see that matter is constantly in flux: that it either deteriorates or gets taken away from us. Although this is obvious, we continually try to deny this reality until we are forced out of the illusion. When our illusions are taken away we often find ourselves lost, angry, confused and depressed. So much intense suffering comes from overly identifying with temporary things.

There was once a famous singer who

performed many concerts and won numerous awards. His albums sold by the millions, and when people heard him sing, many would cry, others would rejoice. One day this famed performer ruptured his vocal chords, and because all of his activities were related to singing, his whole life fell apart. Now he feels totally insignificant. There is no need for him to practice anymore, because there are no more albums, concerts or other appearances. This singer suffers intensely. He has become lost, angry, confused and depressed.

The same is true of one dancer. She was extremely talented and danced so gracefully that it seemed like her feet had wings. This dancer performed the world over, and whenever she wasn't performing, she was practicing her craft. She was shocked to discover that she had gradually developed diabetes. The ironic thing is that her disease never manifested until the peak of her career. Once the disease took root, she became very sick and later lost a leg. Since the amputation, not only can she not dance anymore, but even walking has become excruciating. Life has lost all meaning, and she thinks of herself as a helpless nobody. Consequently, she suffers intensely, and has become lost, angry, confused and depressed.

Speaking of her reminds me of one professional athlete—a star performer in every event he entered. All of his fans and team members loved and respected him, and he was the favorite of all his coaches. Fans practically worshiped him in the stadiums; they stood in the bleachers cheering him, and at his office, stacks of letters and gifts were always there to greet him. Even product manufacturers pursued him, and begged him to advertise their wares. But, even more dear to him than all this adulation was the incredible money he brought home each year, with which he purchased so many indulgences.

Given all the wealth and fame he amassed, it was easy for him to satisfy his voracious sex drive. But, after a physical check up he discovered that he had contracted AIDS. To his surprise, he began to deteriorate rapidly. Within two years, in fact, he was completely bed-ridden. His fans seem to have forgotten him and he rarely receives a visitor. The athlete is suffering intensely. He has become lost, angry, confused and depressed.

He's not unlike one of the nation's most gorgeous models, who had been on the cover of every major magazine. She was not only exquisitely beautiful, but perfectly proportioned as well. All the agencies sought her image. They wished that they could clone her, but instead they paid millions for her to endorse their fashions.

Because of her celebrity status, she received many luxurious perks and gratuities. Designers even welcomed her to keep most of the fashions she modeled for them. Most women became instantly full of envy just looking at her. As for men, when they looked, they could not resist desiring her and undressing her with their eyes. Often she had to be guarded, because there was always the chance that she would be followed.

One day, at the end of a photo shoot, she was raped by her photographer. This incident caused her such trauma that she was never the same again. She developed an eating disorder and began voraciously eating everything in sight. Within a year she gained seventy-five pounds and her whole body became distorted. Her career came to a grinding halt. Not even second-rate modeling agencies would hire her. Her story made her an outcaste, and she suffered intensely. This model became lost, angry, confused and depressed.

There was once an extremely popular comedian. His jokes were the talk of the town, and made people laugh until they cried. The world's best nightclubs and television studios fought over him for bookings. He drew large crowds and could command any salary he wanted. His intelligence and wit were so sharp that he could make the most stern-faced scrooge crack a grin and become jovial. Doctors even wanted to use him in experiments for laugh therapy.

The jokes this comic told could immediately change an atmosphere into whatever effect he desired. It seemed that every news item and life event was just another opportunity to make a brilliant joke. Then one day his twelve-year-old daughter was killed in a car crash. She was his only child, and the object of his complete adoration. Her death was so devastating to him that it made him almost comatose. All the happiness and optimism he was known for vanished like a magician's coin.

He tried to continue making others laugh, but his attempts were futile. He could not even appear on stage. Once, when scheduled to perform for royalty, the comedian burst into tears at the thought of his dead daughter. Word soon got out in the entertainment circuit and he could no longer find employment. Like the other celebrities, this comedian suffered intensely, and like the others he became lost, angry, confused and depressed.

There was once a politician who enjoyed his great seniority because it provided many things for his constituents. He kept getting re-elected. He would go out of his way to find out what the people wanted. He kept those he represented well informed about all issues, except one: his private life. Eventually, it was discovered that he had three mistresses and four illegitimate children. The fact that he was always preaching morality and family values made this discovery even more disturbing to the people. In a few weeks he was impeached and would never be able to return to politics again. This politician became lost, angry, confused and depressed—much like his friend, the brain surgeon.

This particular surgeon was extremely wealthy, and his reputation for successful operations was unparalleled. People the world over contacted him for consultations. Even his own colleagues sought audiences with him, hoping to learn some of his magic. In fact, the demand for his skill and expertise was so great that other brain surgeons lined up waiting to be paired with him for an operation. His hands were so skilled that he could perform the most delicate of operations. This ivy-league doctor was only forty years old with his entire life ahead of him. No one could have predicted how short his future would be.

One day he made a horrendous mistake while operating on a famous patient. He had rushed the operation so that he could watch a television program about his extraordinary career. In his haste, he left a surgical instrument in the patient's brain causing the man to die. The patient's widow sued both the doctor and the hospital, and overnight this famous doctor became infamous, losing not only his money but also his job and his license to practice. Needless to say, this doctor became lost, angry, confused and depressed.

There was once a farmer who had a very large and profitable farm. The soil on his farm was excellent and the climate in the area perfect for agriculture. His plants grew to enormous, record-breaking sizes. The animals this farmer kept seemed very happy. The farmer's wife and five children were very proud of their dad, after all, their grandfather and great grandfather had all been farmers, but of all of his predecessors, their dad was the best.

Then, one day the entire village surrounding the farm experienced a drought, and his farm was particularly affected. That was the beginning of his end. Within a few seasons, the

farmer went bankrupt and lost everything.
Even his most basic tools had to be auctioned
off to pay his creditors. The farmer had always
heard that things like this could happen, but in
spite of these warnings he became lost, angry,
confused and depressed.

It is amazing how fragile everyone's situation in the material world is, and it can be
frightening to consider how people can be such
high achievers with wonderful things happen-
ing in their lives, and then one day, without
warning, they can experience a tragic, irre-
versible change.

Even one who leads a normal, uneventful
life will inevitably experience death—the
great equalizer—and with death, a loss of all
their fame, beauty, talent and security.

I am looking closer at my own life to see
what attachments and illusions I have struc-
tured my life around. My false ego keeps me in
denial about the limitations of my material
success, achievements and security. Thus, I, the
Beggar, am pleading to the Lord to never allow
me to take for granted any such material
achievements or success or security. I, the
Beggar, constantly pray to the Lord to allow
me to focus on the unfoldment of my eternal
spiritual nature.

Just as I finished my prayer, I heard some
angelic beings laughing. Then one of them
spoke and broke the laughter. "You actually
expect to avoid being drunk with power? Do
you really think you can escape the clutches of
chasing after fame so easily? Beloved, haven't

you realized it yet? All those tragic personalities whose misfortunes you were meditating on were you yourself in different lifetimes.

"We have watched you with great amusement lifetime after lifetime as you became engrossed in your temporary identities, trying to mold each of them into the perfect success story. But this time you have set a new precedence of illusion, for this time you are imagining yourself as a Guru and savior to the masses. The funniest part is, what you don't realize is that all of those souls you are guiding and helping are but fragments of your own desires and illusions.

"Once you discard your false ego and abandon all your various attachments, you will finally be able to wholeheartedly surrender to our worshipable Lord. Then you will be able to jump over all the hurdles of your desires, and find true contentment in the Lord in your heart.

"But if it takes you a little longer, don't worry. Although your behavior all these lifetimes has been most eccentric, we will not abandon you. You see, we have been instructed to stay close by and keep an eye on you, just slightly out of sight of your material vision, until the time when you are ready for us to escort you back home.

"It's true, you have many outrageous delusions of grandeur, and yet, by God's grace, the time for your homecoming is not far away. The best part is, the homecoming will be real cause for your jubilation. At that point, you will realize your greatest fantasy. At that point, you will fully re-enter the Divine Romance, and you will never again become lost, angry, confused or depressed."

Meditation 14

An opportunity to embrace the miracle

My soul is very patient, but after giving me pure love for many lifetimes, he has become impatient with my slow progress and delayed responses to his guidance and encouragement. In the meantime, both my subtle and gross bodies have become equally frustrated and disappointed with my undermining of our progress. Every day, so many people break their resolutions, vows, pledges and plans, just because of their lack of focus and perseverance. These people lack determination and are so impersonal that they eventually acquire improper mindsets, and "accidentally" become recaptured by bad habits.

At weekly meetings around the world, millions of people pledge to give up drugs, alcohol, cigarettes, improper eating, duplicity, deviousness and a host of other vices. But most of them get distracted and resume their old patterns. Some of these relapsers go into denial; others get so frustrated with their own cowardice that they consider committing suicide. I decided to raise these concerns directly with my soul:

"I am eager to go beyond all these boundaries and enter the true freedom that is my actual birthright," I confided in my soul. "But I need further guidance in how to overcome these last remaining blocks. Please, dear soul, give me additional support. I promise, I will not disappoint you again, for now I am a much more desperate Beggar."

My soul spoke out sharply but lovingly, "There is nothing new for you to hear, but let me reiterate some points from our previous sessions. First, you must always keep the supreme goal in mind. Begin each activity with the end in mind! On any path, there are always blocks, tests and challenges, but you can see each of these obstacles as an opportunity to embrace another miracle.

"Every challenge you face is just another chance to go faster toward our divine integration and our sublime reunion with the Supreme. But to accomplish this, you must see everyone and everything as a messenger or message from God.

"There are no such things as accidents.

Accidents are only incidents you don't yet understand, or that are out of your control. However, nothing escapes the control and understanding of our almighty, worshipable Lord.

"The Lord is unlimitedly merciful and loving—and He is always inviting us to return to His divine abode. Just accept this unflinchingly, and you will learn from all people and occurrences in your life.

"All you have to do is look constantly for what you are to learn from each encounter, and remain mindful that there is no such thing as an accident. The all-knowing, all-merciful Supreme Lord has allowed every experience that has entered your life. He and no one else is the Supreme Controller. If you can capture this mood consistently, then your success is guaranteed."

My soul looked at me with great compassion and continued, "You must chant and pray ceaselessly, because the mind is so vicious and mischievous. Your mind will constantly search for ways to draw attention to itself, and as soon as you relax, your mischievous mind will once again rule."

"But my mind is so much stronger than me, how can I ever hope to conquer it?

"There is only one way to master the mind, and that is through constant prayer, chanting, meditation, affirmations and most importantly through visualizations. Visualizations must accompany all your other practices, for they will remind you of what you are to achieve or are achieving, and why you are doing every-thing else."

My soul looked at me with pity. "Give up all desires for fame—want only truth and service. When you are eager for personal fame, you lose proper perspective.

"Fame seekers will overlook important opportunities, and will devote their time and energies to unhealthy and superfluous concerns. They will confuse evil for good and deny good for evil. Such persons will only look for opportunities that grant them personal pleasure and will therefore become insensitive, utilitarian opportunists. Instead of looking for truth, righteousness and service, they will simply look for ways to use other people and facilities for their own benefit.

"Anyone who remains attached to fame and adoration will lose the determination and ability to obtain the goal of returning back home. Before you accept any thought into your being, qualify all of your reflections. In fact, everything that comes to you, must be quali-fied. Otherwise, do not accept or identify with it.

"In other words, constantly evaluate each idea to see if the thought, word or possible action being considered is truly in the interest of our short and long-term goals.

"The tendency of the mind is to try to sneak things through our barriers by present-ing an attractive *façade*. When such reflections do not help move us faster toward the Godhead, they should be immediately rejected. In this way the intelligence will not so easily accept something that is detrimental to its elevation.

"If one is selective about what to accept, success will be guaranteed. Otherwise stagnation and failure are assured.

My soul paused in deep reflection before speaking again. "You must look to the future while learning from the past. Try to remember how you became locked into surrendering to improper mindsets, temptations and bad habits so many times in the past. Recapture those experiences, remember how you were enticed, and remember how you rationalized giving into your lower nature.

"Remember all of the attractive aspects that convinced you to accept the deviation. Most important, you must remember how foolish, sad and depressed you felt after you once again lost your focus and glided downward. If you can remember the suffering you feel after failing a test, you will be more alert to avert such failures in the future.

"Instead of succumbing to them, use these experiences for growth, and remember how wonderful you felt every time you scored well on your tests and didn't give into illusions. Remember the joy of making serious spiritual advancement, and know that simply sustaining this will assure your eventual attainment of total victory.

"You must stop identifying yourself as the physical body, senses, mind, intelligence, false ego and material time. Yes the body, senses, mind, intelligence and false ego are real, but they are only a temporary reality. In other words, you are the temporary reality, but I am the eternal reality.

"You must surrender and give up this temporary identity, so that we can fully integrate into the one eternal reality. You see, beloved, you are not who you think you are. For lifetimes you have accepted this temporary reality and categorically denied my existence. But this has only prolonged the pain, illusion and separation that keeps you bound in misery. So again, you must surrender, and die to live!

"Give up this temporary identification so that we can merge into one fantastic, complete, blissful and eternal entity, fully energized in serving the Divine Couple in our original mood. By allowing this, you will not lose anything. Rather, you will gain total existence and cognizance, for you are really a reflection of me, and I am you in your most perfect manifestation.

"By giving up your material conception of time you ultimately allow us to move faster in becoming whole and complete.

"The material concept of time exists in relationship to various material commodities and material bodies. All material things are part of the temporary reality.

"All of the many rituals and rules you have been instructed to follow and all of the suffering you have undergone in many bodies has simply been fleeting moments for us connected with eternal time.

"Beloved, this means that if you can once

and for all follow my instructions and maintain the proper focus, perseverance and determination, we will be victorious in a flash, residing in full splendor and eternal love in the spiritual world.

"Do not feel that your task is too difficult or allow yourself to slow down. We are finishing up our last challenges and obstacles. The only problem is that you are forgetting to embrace the miracle. Actually, everything else will slip through your fingers, so this time, embrace the miracle."

"*Your unalloyed devotees want nothing, because they know that within You is everything... My dear Lord Damodara, when will I become such a devotee?*"

Meditation 15

Desire nothing and receive everything

My dear Lord Damodara, You can only be bound by pure love. Your devotees are totally surrendered to You in love, therefore You have surrendered Yourself fully to them and allowed them to capture You.

Whenever such devotees are offered any type of boon, they repeatedly refuse, asking only to always remember You, never forget You, and always be able to hear about or serve You and Your helpers. Your unalloyed devotees want nothing, because they know that everything is within You.

The saintly King Mucukunda killed

Kalayavana with scorching flames from his eyes when he awoke in the cave from his very long slumber. Upon seeing Lord Krishna, Mucukunda did not know who He was. But after Krishna explained Himself, He offered the King any boon he might request. This is when King Mucukunda offered very heartfelt prayers and told his beloved Lord: "O all powerful One, I desire no boon other than that most eagerly sought by those free of material desires: service to Your lotus feet!" King Mucukunda continued: "O Hari, What enlightened person who worships You, the giver of liberation, would choose a boon that causes his own bondage?" *(Srimad Bhagavatam 10.51.55)*

My dear Lord Damodara, when will I become such a devotee?

Thousands of kings and princes were imprisoned by the demon Jarasandha. The destitution of their extended imprisonment offered the kings and princes a great "opportunity" to remember the Lord. This was an opportunity that they gladly took advantage of. Thus, when Lord Krishna approached the royal order in their decrepit state, they spontaneously offered the following prayers:

"We pray for Your Lordship to favor us by instructing us how to engage in the transcendental loving service of Your lotus feet, so that we may never forget our eternal relationship with Your Lordship. We do not want liberation from the entanglement of material existence. By Your will, we may take birth in any species of life; it does not matter. We simply pray that we never forget Your lotus feet under any circumstances." *(Krishna book, chapter 73)*

My dear Lord Damodara, when will I become such a devotee?

After Maharaja Prthu had perfectly performed ninety-nine horse sacrifices, Lord Vishnu appeared before him in the sacrificial arena and offered Prthu any benediction he desired. Prthu Maharaja simply responded:

"My dear Lord, I do not wish to have the benediction of merging into Your existence, a benediction in which there is no existence of the nectarean beverage of Your lotus feet. I want the benediction of at least one million ears, for thus I may be able to hear about the glories of Your lotus feet from the mouths of Your pure devotees. My dear Lord, I do not need any other benediction but the opportunity to hear from the mouth of your pure devotee." *(Srimad Bhagavatam 4.20.24-25)*

My dear Lord Damodara, when will I become such a devotee?

The exalted, pure devotee of the Lord, King Rantideva, once performed a forty-eight day fast. On the 49th day, when he was about to break his fast, several different guests started appearing. Although these guests were varied in many respects, all of them had something in common: Each of them was hungry for Rantideva's food.

Without hesitation, Rantideva selflessly served each of the guests that appeared, one after the other. Even though his own hunger brought him near death, he still enthusiastically gave out not only all of his food, but also every drop of his water. Fortunately for the King, these guests turned out to be demigods in disguise. They had manifested themselves to test Rantideva's devotion and his sense of duty to the kingly order. Each demigod who came to Rantideva was so impressed with the King's selfless love and compassion that they offered him any boon he desired. Rantideva, however, felt no inclination to ask anything of them. His only request was that he might always think lovingly of Lord Krishna.

My dear Lord Damodara, when will I become such a devotee?

A great devotee and former schoolmate of Lord Krishna's named Sudama Vipra lived with his wife in a very impoverished condition. Although Sudama saw no value or necessity of asking the Lord for material rewards, due to his wife's repeated requests, Sudama Vipra agreed to go visit the Lord. On his way there, Sudama excitedly thought, "If I go to Dwaraka to the Lord's palace, I shall personally see the Lord. Even if I don't ask any material benefit from Him, what a great opportunity it will be to see Lord Krishna."

Although Sudama never asked the Lord for anything, Krishna bestowed upon Sudama's wife opulent facilities that far exceeded the luxury enjoyed by the King of Heaven. Sudama didn't even see these great boons until after his long foot journey back home from Dwaraka. In gratitude for the Lord relieving his wife's anxieties, Sudama Vipra prayed aloud: "I pray to have the friendship of Lord Krishna and to engage in His service and to surrender fully unto Him in love and affection, lifetime after lifetime.

"I do not want any opulence. I only desire not to forget His service. I simply wish to be associated with His pure devotees. May my mind and activities be always engaged in His service." *(Srimad Bhagavatam 10.81)*

My dear Lord Damodara, when will I become such a devotee?

When Krishna and Balarama entered Mathura, they had a few notable encounters with other citizens before coming upon another Sudama. This Sudama was a florist who went daily to the market with his bouquets of fresh flowers. Upon seeing Their Lordships, Sudama warmly greeted Krishna and Balarama with various services and offerings. To reciprocate these loving gestures, Lord Krishna then offered Sudama a benediction. In response to this, Sudama simply begged of the Lord the ability to remain His eternal servant. "May I remain in Your constant devotional service, and by so doing render good to all other living creatures."

My dear Lord Damodara, when will I become such a devotee?

After Prahlad Maharaja pacified Lord Nrsimhadeva with prayers, the Lord asked Prahlad to request a benediction from Him. Prahlad immediately became somewhat hurt that the Lord would suggest he was a merchant with ulterior motives for rendering service.

Prahlad then went on to explain how distasteful it is to ask a material reward of one's beloved Lord, Who has already given His devotee so many things, including life, cognizance and countless other facilities. When Lord Nrsimhadeva insisted Prahlad request something of Him, Prahlad expressed the desire to have all material aspirations removed from his heart. *(Srimad Bhagavatam 7.10.1-8)*

My dear Lord Damodara, when will I become such a devotee?

After killing so many yaksa demons, Dhruva approached Kuvera to ask for forgiveness. In reaction, Kuvera instructed Dhruva about devotional service and then offered to grant him any benediction he desired. In response, Dhruva begged that he might have unflinching faith in and remembrance of the Supreme Personality of Godhead. "I request this of you, Kuvera, because any fortunate soul who has developed firm faith and remembrance of the Lord can cross over the ocean of nescience very easily, although it is very difficult for others to cross." *(Srimad Bhagavatam 4.12.1-8)*

My dear Lord Damodara, when will I become such a devotee?

Kholavecha Sridhara was a greatly renounced and austere devotee of the Lord. For the sake of His pastimes, Lord Chaitanya would purposely go to Kholavecha to buy banana leaves and playfully quarrel over money or the quality of his wares. During the Maha-prakasa pastime, Lord Chaitanya asked

Kholavecha to request a boon and Kholavecha replied:

"May the Brahmana who gave me coins for my banana leaves be my Lord birth after birth. May that Brahmana who quarreled with me over price be my eternal Master. May He give me His lotus feet to worship forever more."

Overcome with love, Kholavecha Sridhara spoke these words again and again as he wept.

In response, Lord Chaitanya smiled: "I will give you a great Kingdom. I will make you a great King." But Kholavecha looked at his Lord, "I don't want any of that. You please become My master and I will sing Your name."

My dear Lord Damodara, when will I become such a devotee?

During the same *Maha-prakasa* lila, after bestowing boons to Kholavecha Sridhara, Lord Chaitanya began to gently sway His head and repeat the name "Nada, Nada, Nada." He then spoke to Advaita Acarya: "Acarya! Ask of Me what You need."

The Acarya replied, "My prayers have already been answered my Lord." Lord Chaitanya appreciated this answer with a thunderous roar that drowned out all other sound.

The Lord then revealed to Murari Gupta His identity as Lord Ramacandra, and said to Murari, "You may ask Me for any boon."

Sri Murari replied: "My Lord, I do not want anything that You have not already bestowed. Just grant me one wish, that I may sing only of Your glories. Put me into any situation of Your choosing birth after birth. Just simply allow me to remember You and serve You in the association of Your servitors." Murari continued: "O my Lord, please never place me in a position where I may deviate from the Absolute Truth or forget that You are the Supreme Lord and that I am Your eternal servant. Wherever You descend accompanied by Your eternal associates, I desire to be there as Your insignificant servitor."

My dear Lord Damodara, please force me to give up all last traces of the false ego so that I can also become one of your unalloyed devotees. These devotees want nothing, because they know that everything exists within You.

Meditation 16

The Lord's mercy is greater than His law

The laws that govern our lives are material, metaphysical and spiritual. When we abide by these laws there is great auspiciousness, but when we break any category of law, there may be serious consequences—especially in the sphere of spirituality.

Of course, laws are necessary to inform people and guide them in how they are held accountable in their status as human beings. However, despite the fact that a law is in place, a judicial authority may sometimes introduce the mercy factor. This mercy factor does not negate the law, but it allows one to escape or not be accountable for the full import of the law.

The mercy factor is a constant occurrence in the spiritual paradigm, especially in our present age of *Kali yuga*, or the age of quarrel and hypocrisy.

Normally, there are three categories of persons who are able to go back to Godhead. One of these categories is the *nitya-siddha:* personalities who are eternally liberated. These great souls are never conditioned; they enter the material world by choice from the spiritual world, disguised as ordinary people.

Being eternally liberated, and thus exceedingly compassionate, *nitya-siddhas* are on a mission to reclaim souls back to the Godhead. When they finish their work, they may go back to their home in the spiritual world, or go on another mission for the Supreme.

The second category of persons going to the spiritual kingdom is the *sadhana-siddhas.* These are persons who have been materially conditioned, but have gradually obtained purity by their serious spiritual practices.

The third category of persons who can return home is known as the *kripa-siddhas.* These are persons who have received special mercy and blessings from either the Lord or one of the Lord's agents.

In all three of these categories, of course, the mercy factor is present. But this mercy factor is especially dominant in the case of the *kripa-siddha.* In this case, mercy is far more prominent than the rule of law.

In this age of Kali, people are unlucky, quarrelsome and misguided, and so prone to sinful life that special mercy is greatly needed. We are therefore all extremely fortunate that in this age, the Lord's mercy often supercedes His law.

In the Bhagavad-gita *(9.30-31)*, we find that even if someone has an accidental fall down, although he or she has utterly dishonored a spiritual principle, he or she is to be considered saintly, and is worthy of everyone's respect. Such a person should never continue his mistaken behavior, but as long as he can rectify and purify himself, he is considered to be on the saintly platform.

The Supreme Lord knows that the neophyte devotee may take some of Maya's allurements and challenges for granted, and may therefore be temporarily caught off guard. But, while the lawbreaking habits of a neophyte is certainly subject to repercussion, the mercy that the Lord extends will still predominate His law.

In essence, we are all similar to the Lord in that we are made in God's image, and of the same divine quality. Therefore, we are endowed with free will and have some minute degree of independence. The Lord's laws never interfere with our free will. However, out of grace, the Lord often extends Himself and goes far outside of His law to help a floundering devotee.

This might be called a case of divine intervention. One classic example is that of Kala Krishnadas. Demonstrating the potency of Maya, this devotee actually left the Lord's association to pursue sense gratification with a group of gypsies. To save Kala Krishnadas, the Lord personally intervened by literally dragging Krishnadas away from that sinful community. The Lord's rescue of Kala Krishnadas is evidence that His mercy is greater than His law.

Normally, by spiritual law a renounced monk is not eager to associate with persons engrossed in worldly habits. Yet, despite the fact that He was in the renounced order, Lord Chaitanya gave His mercy to the three kings Patraparudra, Ramananda Roy, and Pundarika. Although all three of these royal personalities were rulers in material culture, they were also great devotees full of love for the Lord. Because of this, the Lord pushed aside all sense of law and etiquette to receive His devotees' affectionate loving service, and He eagerly returned that love according to their desires. How wonderful it is to once again see that the Lord's mercy is far greater than His law.

Seeing how degraded the Age of Kali had and would continue to become, the pure devotees Narada Muni and Advaita Acarya petitioned the Lord to do something special. They suggested that instead of the Lord sending an empowered representative to rectify fallen souls, that He must break traditional spiritual law and etiquette and descend Himself to give out special mercy because the problems of Kali were so severe.

Taking their advice, Krishna descended as Lord Caitanya Mahaprabhu and then arranged things such that all living entities would be exposed to the Lord's potent mercy and love with or without qualification.

Lord Caitanya put aside the law to save Gopinath Pattanayaka after his devotee made an appeal. The Lord also converted the vicious sinners Jagai and Madhai, who had regularly broken all types of laws. Although those sinful brothers had disregarded material, metaphysical and spiritual laws, Chaitanya Mahaprabhu put aside karmic law and liberated them, giving them His highest causeless mercy.

Mahaprabhu even broke etiquette and gave His mercy to a young, austere brahmana boy, a Mohammedan tailor and even a dog in Srivas Thakur's house. How fortunate the living entities are that the Lord's mercy is even greater than His laws.

Although the fallen brahmana Ajamila had committed so many sins against innocents, because he called on the Lord's holy name offenselessly at the time of death, he was given liberation.

Putana is another example of a demon who came to attack Krishna and was instead checked from her devious activity and then awarded liberation. By law, Putana and all the other demons who came to kill Krishna should have been sentenced to long periods on the hellish planets, but despite their demonic intent, the Lord's mercy was far greater than His law.

Jesus broke etiquette by washing the feet of his disciples. Similarly, Lord Krishna also washed the feet of many devotees at a Raja-surya sacrifice. Krishna also washed the feet of Sudama Vipra, and in an extreme act of humility and breach of natural order, the Supreme Lord became known as Paratha Sarathi when He drove Arjuna's chariot in the battle of Kuruksetra.

All these orthodox spiritual laws were put aside by the Lord to demonstrate a more important principle: that Krishna will gladly do whatever is necessary to protect and facilitate His unalloyed devotees—including becoming His devotees' servant. How wonderful it is that the Lord's mercy is greater than His law.

The spiritual master and any of the Lord's pure representatives are themselves spiritual "brokers" or intermediaries. Often these compassionate souls appeal to the Lord to extend His mercy far above the limit of His laws. We find examples of this in the life of Jesus.

Jesus Christ converted the prostitute Mary Magdelane and turned her into a first class servant of the Lord. He also pleaded the case for the criminals who died on the cross with Him to be able to enter with Him into paradise.

The Prophet Mohammed appealed to the Lord for Him to grant special mercy and forgiveness to those who were having sex with their mothers, and those who were killing their female babies. The prophet even pleaded to the Lord on behalf of the slaves and orphans, that they too might receive proper guidance and mercy.

Lord Buddha intervened to bring mercy to those who had gone astray with unhealthy animal sacrifices. He even put aside certain Vedic laws that were causing confusion and abuse. How wonderful to see how the Lord's servants and the Lord's mercy are far greater than His law.

Normally, according to spiritual law, as soon as one takes birth he is obliged to all of his forefathers, the demigods, the sun, the moon and many other superiors. To fulfill these obligations, there are so many prayers and rituals one would have to perform to appease their various creditors. But a person who takes shelter of pure devotional service is relieved of all these obligations, and is no longer indebted to these superiors.

Because bhakti (devotion) waters the root of the devotional creeper and satisfies the Supreme Godhead, nourishment of all the Lord's parts and parcels is automatically achieved.

Bhakti is so strong that it is even as great or greater than God! This is because the Lord allows the exchange of pure loving relationships to transcend all formalities. The devotee in pure loving relationship can connect with the Supreme and even capture Him, because God, seated in the heart of that devotee, realizes his desire to render pure and loving service to his Beloved.

As I thought gratefully about the Lord's causeless mercy, I thought of my Guru and all that he had done in the past to smash the illusions of my false ego. Then, just as I thought of my Guru, his voice broke into my thoughts.

"This, beloved," said my spiritual master, "is the nature of the spiritual world. Laws are transcended because there are actually no lawbreakers, no barriers to giving and receiving love, and because mercy is shared and extended to its highest degree in a continual expression by the Divine Couple."

"My darling, although sometimes it seems almost impossible to do so, subdue the imaginings of your false ego and keep honoring all spiritual laws. In this way, you will soon be able to live eternally in the land without laws, where pure love and mercy is all we know and associate with."

Meditation 17

Become possessed in transcendental culture

To day my spiritual mentor discussed with me how we have experienced so many encounters together in Krishna's service. Sometimes I've had the privilege of assisting him nicely and other times I have made myself a serious disturbance.

In his loving appraisal, my Guru told me that I have sometimes transcended my many blockages and advanced in consciousness, while other times I have just narrowly escaped devastation.

"Each time you have passed a test," he said, "I have been very happy to see your

"*fear nothing, desire nothing and ask for nothing except to be a pure vessel for God's love!*"

success, for this has pushed you forward a great distance and prepared you nicely for the next challenge."

"I know you have rarely gotten a chance to relax," he said to me with a caring glint in his eye, "before I presented you with another test, but this is just my way of bringing you home more quickly, and preparing you for your greatest test."

"But what is that greatest of tests?" I asked him.

"Your greatest test is that you must now become totally possessed by the Godhead. It is not just a matter of hearing or speaking the philosophy. It is not even a matter of just living theology. You must become engulfed and devoured by every aspect of the culture of transcendence.

"That means, everywhere you look you must be able to see God's love, mercy and protection. Every thought that enters your mind must be either directly or indirectly connected to devotional meditation. Everywhere you go, you must not only take God with you, but you must see that place as a rendezvous site where you will meet the Lord in His full splendor. Even your eating, sleeping, mating and defending must be only for the Lord; otherwise, you are to cease these activities.

"All nonsensical talking should also cease, because unless your words become a catalyst for glorifying the Supreme Lord and His servants you will fail to reach the goal."

"But," I questioned my master, "the road to success seems so narrow, and the pitfalls on that road are innumerable."

He replied: "The secret is: fear nothing, desire nothing and ask for nothing except to be God's pure and loving vessel. If you really desire this, Lord Krishna will make it possible. However, this can only happen by becoming a genuine lover of everyone you encounter."

We were silent for a few moments, then my spiritual mentor revealed more knowledge. "In the past you have possessed too many fears and had too many aspirations that have clouded your ability to transcend. You have kept asking your guides for help, but made all your requests so conditional that you hampered your own success. Now you must reach the stage of being fully detached from all happiness or distress, fame or infamy. You must eliminate all distinctions between friend and enemy, and never become the enemy of your enemies."

"But how can this attitude be achieved?"

"When you experience boons, achievements or happiness, you must simply realize that God's mercy is causeless. Similarly, when friends help to support or glorify you, honestly feel that you have done nothing to deserve this praise. Conversely, when setbacks occur, no matter how extreme they seem, again thank the Lord for His causeless mercy.

"Regard all these distresses as only token punishments that have been minimized by God's mercy. When people attack you, envision even this as a wonderful learning opportunity.

"Above all, you must always look for ways to be a better servant of all those who enter your midst."

"But how can I do that?"

"As you immerse yourself in the culture of transcendence, you will learn to avoid being pulled into duality, and instead remain fixed in receiving and experiencing Krishna's love!"

I contemplated my mentor's wise words. "Could I really experience all this in just one lifetime?"

My dear Guru began to explain. "Being totally possessed with God means to see all life as sacred. Every living entity exists in the body of God. As the Bible says, "having joyfully entertained guests, they hosted angels unaware." But not only angels are significant; actually, all beings are of the same quality—all beings belong to God—the only difference is their level of realization and empowerment."

"But what about those entities who seem to be running away from God with all their might?" I asked him.

"Let those entities be an example to you of the zeal you should use in running toward the Lord. Do exactly as they are doing, but run just as quickly in the other direction, with full absorption and dedication to the Supreme."

"But I am so often troubled by my mind."

"Yes it's true. No matter how perfect your actions, you must also eventually perfect your sight and your vision."

"Is that ever really possible?"

"Of course it is. By honoring God's sacred presence in every being you encounter, your sight will become perfected. And this will keep you from being slowed by the abundance of dualities and distractions."

My master and I walked together along a narrow, muddy path. Then my spiritual mentor turned and stopped in his tracks.

"There is one thing you can do that will make everything easier for you. You must maintain intense spiritual greed. Just like a man who is dying of thirst or starvation; nothing will occupy his mind except the vision of food and water. Such a person will have singular focus. Nothing else will appeal to him or give him solace. Similarly, the true aspirant who honestly wants the highest spiritual attainment must have this level of intensity. For a spiritually greedy transcendentalist, nothing outside the Lord's service is sufficient to satisfy his soul."

My master continued: "Please try to understand how such a dying person will be extremely conscious of the way he uses every moment. Each second that he's deprived of food and water will jeopardize his entire existence. The clock is running out, and the dying man is very clear about this. Possessed by his cravings, he wastes not one single second, but instead uses every bit of strength he can muster to desperately try to secure some sustenance."

"But if I behave like that, everyone will think I've gone crazy."

"Developing this intense absorption is beyond the realm of rationality and normalcy. Forget everyone else's opinion. This is between you and God—between you and your destiny!

"Don't you remember the example of Madhavendra Puri? All the philosophers of his age and even all of his friends and relatives thought that he had gone mad. But these opinions were of no concern to him, for he was possessed with pursuing Krishna's complete love and association. Even though he felt himself unworthy and considered the task impossible, still he sought the Lord with vigorous determination."

He continued: "Haridas Thakur is another example. Although flogged and tortured in so many marketplaces, Haridas Thakur never got distracted or resentful; he persevered in his faith with complete fixedness. Of course, Bhakta Prahlad also exemplifies this."

"The boy's own father tried to kill him in so many vicious ways. He attempted to poison Prahlad's food, boil him in a vat of oil, trap him in a pit of snakes, and pierce him with tridents, swords and spears. Prahlad was even thrown from a cliff and trampled by wild elephants, yet Prahlad took full shelter of Krishna's Holy Name, and thus he felt absolutely no fear, pain or disturbance. Both Prahlad Maharaja and Haridas Thakur were fully absorbed in spiritual transcendence, and thus oblivious to pain and even death."

I was overwhelmed: "But Prahlad came from a dynasty present millions of years ago and even Haridas lived in another era. These things don't happen anymore."

"Of course they do," my Guru argued. "Besides, Haridas Thakur was an associate of Lord Chaitanya living only 500 years ago. Also in that era was Nrsimhananda brahmacari. Don't you recall how he became possessed with the spirit of Lord Chaitanya, and thus became endowed with paranormal powers?

"And what about the power of possession demonstrated by Kholavecha Sridhara and Sudama Vipra? Have you also forgotten them? Both of them were extremely poor, yet they had no demands, material desires or disturbances. Those two had insufficient food, shabby clothing, inadequate shelter and even poor health. They had nothing but genuine devotion to offer the Lord, but Krishna accepted all of their offerings."

"Not only did Krishna fully accept their offerings, but He personally presented Himself before them to accept their submissions and to get their association. So pleased was the Lord by their devotion, that He became intoxicated in full gratitude to receive these devotees' offerings. Because these unalloyed devotees were fully possessed and absorbed in the Lord's meditation, Krishna Himself hankered to have their association.

"Reflect deeply on this," my spiritual mentor suggested. "Reflect on such servants of the Lord like Buddha, and how while meditating under the *Bodhi* tree, Buddha became totally possessed in transcendence, and became determined to remain there until he received enlightenment."

"There are so many cases of this kind of possessed absorption. Consider, for instance, Prophet Mohammed. Despite all kinds of attacks and challenges, this exalted soul remained determined to do God's will. Similarly, the Biblical figure Abraham was so possessed with pleasing and serving God that he was ready, if necessary, to sacrifice his own son.

"And surely, you remember the examples of Jesus Christ and Vasudeva-datta—two souls who were so self-sacrificing that they were willing to take all of the sins and sufferings of the world onto themselves so that others could be purified and return back to Godhead.

"But, above all, you must not forget Krishna's topmost servants in the spiritual world: the gopis. I'm sure you recall that when Krishna left the gopis after the rasa dance, they became completely possessed and intoxicated as they searched for Him. Some gopis began talking to and embracing the trees, and others pretended to be Krishna.

"As for Srimati Radharani, She is always so fully possessed, bathing in Govinda´s love, that She often cannot eat, sleep or dress Herself properly. Sometimes to calm Herself in Krishna's absence, She even talks to the bumblebees, thinking Krishna is present or reachable in this way. All the gopis have lovingly given themselves over to Krishna and He has given Himself totally to them.

"Being fully possessed by the culture of unconditional love and service, the gopis are like people who are literally blindly in love, but thousands of times more intense. In such a state of mind everything connected with one's lover becomes stimulating and intoxicating. Because one can never get enough of the lover's attention and association, being together or being separate from their love object is almost equally painful. Going anywhere or doing anything is depressing and unfulfilling if not in the association of one's lover.

"Even the most wonderful happenings are hellish if one cannot share the experience with his lover. At the same time, the most challenging and hellish experiences become totally sublime if one is in the company of his or her beloved. In both the waking and sleeping states, one's thoughts are totally centered around one's lover. Sometimes a lover laughs or cries, deliriously as thoughts of the beloved come into his consciousness. This is because nothing can equal the pleasure given by one's lover."

My spiritual mentor's gaze seemed to penetrate me: "These are the thoughts and actions of those possessed by the culture of transcendence. My son, this state of being can only be accomplished if you become totally free of false ego and become a pure and genuine, deep lover."

"Souls who enter this stage of loving so intensely understand the formula of first fully emptying one's self in order to be spiritually full. Thus, their presence in the world is never burdensome or unnecessary. Actually, it is the presence of these souls alone that can change the course of history. But this is only because these great souls have always applied one transcendental secret: to fear nothing, desire nothing and ask for nothing except to be a pure vessel for God's love!

"My dear beloved, in your aspirations to cultivate true devotion you have done very well most of the time. Now prepare for the greatest and most wonderful encounter: Fear nothing, desire nothing and ask for nothing except to become a pure vessel for God's love. In this way, become the deepest lover by becoming totally possessed in transcendental culture. We have been waiting for you beloved, so don't delay."

"When I try to
calculate all
that you've done
for me, I am
bursting with
gratitude. But
above all, Srila
Prabhupada,
I thank you for
arranging my
rescue!"

Meditation 18

Thank you for arranging my rescue

My dear Eternal Father and Spiritual Master, Srila Prabhupada:

Lately I have been reflecting more intensely on how fortunate I am, and thousands of other souls on this planet are, to have met and personally served you, or to have been influenced by your glorious teachings. The guidance and encouragement you gave to so many of us is incomparable!

I like to personalize my reflections, so lately I have been wondering what my fate might have been if you had not so gracefully come into my life. I am bursting with gratitude as I try to calculate what you've done for me. But above all, I thank you for arranging my rescue!

If I had not met you, Srila Prabhupada, perhaps I would be the Dean at a University somewhere, overseeing an institution that creates sophisticated animals. Each year, universities are becoming more and more degraded as they teach and campaign for relativism and massive data collecting. True morality, integrity and ethics have become as rare in higher education as the preservation of genuine wisdom. Students as well as professors "know" so much but understand so little. And, like the lifestyles of four-legged animals, they live simply for refining the indulgences of eating, sleeping, mating and defending. When I try to calculate all that you've done for me, I am bursting with gratitude. But above all, Srila Prabhupada, I thank you for arranging my rescue!

If I had not met you, perhaps I would be a politician, traveling the four corners of the earth to represent some sovereign political party or government, while actually just representing myself. Today's world is flooded with cheating politicians who speak and live lies as they smile at the public. Duplicity is their breakfast, exploitation is their lunch and promiscuity is their dinner. Most politicians have poor character, and thus they lack true commitment to their constituents and lack the courage to be principle centered. When I try to calculate all that you've done for me, I am overwhelmed with gratitude. But above all, Srila Prabhupada, I thank you for arranging my rescue!

If I had not met you, Your Divine Grace, I might have pursued a business career in corporate America. If so, I would probably be sitting somewhere in a plush, high rise office building, slowly dying with no clue to the purpose of life. A premature death would be almost guaranteed for me as every day I would be dying of stress, boredom, depression and frustration while trying to get various promotions. I can also imagine how unhappy I would have been to have such a big family that I would have to use almost every waking minute plotting how to make more money to provide for their material desires.

I can reflect on how difficult it would be living in a big house, which would be like a prison, with a high mortgage and security problems. I would be like a slave to that house, and have to work night and day to pay for and keep the house in good condition. When I try to calculate all that your teachings have done for me, I am bursting with total gratitude. But above all, Srila Prabhupada, I thank you for arranging my rescue!

If I had not met you, Srila Prabhupada, there is little doubt that I would have been a civil rights leader, totally absorbed in racial issues. Being relatively smart and sincere, eventually it would have occurred to me that almost everyone's rights are being exploited. This would have created even more confusion as I considered: "Should I fight for women's rights, animal rights, employees' rights, veterans' rights, unborn children's rights, elderly people's rights, handicapped people's rights or whose?"

But often, while different sovereign groups campaign to demand various rights, they are not truly concerned with the problems, needs and rights of so many other people. More often, their demands for various rights overlooks the universal duties and obligations we have as non-material entities. In the process of strategizing for one's material rights, one generally disregards his or her spiritual responsibilities, commitments and obligations. Thus, when I try to calculate all you have done for me, I am overwhelmed with gratitude. But above all, Srila Prabhupada, I have to thank you for arranging my rescue!

If I had not met you, perhaps I would have been a leader or figurehead in a religious or psychic order, becoming more and more intoxicated by my own spheres of influence. If this were my lot, I am sure that I would have begun busily pursuing mundane popularity and mystic powers while believing myself a savior. Although it may not have looked that way, surely I would have been using spirituality to acquire a material empire for myself and family, and using God for my own name and fame.

Since this sort of adoration is very addictive, I am sure that I would not have stopped there. Rather I would have begun using not only God, but also His church, His people and watered down versions of His teachings as leverage for my own worldly fame and recognition. While telling people about God, I would surely have become sectarian and fanatical in order to enhance my own power and prestige. When I try to calculate all that you've done for me, and how you've saved me, I am overwhelmed with loving gratitude. But above all, Srila Prabhupada, I thank you for arranging my rescue!

Your grace alone has given me the rare opportunity to live most of my life as a celibate monk, to vigorously preach and in this way please the Supreme Personality of Godhead. Not only have you introduced me to the Absolute Truth as a Person, but you have also introduced me to other rare and exalted personalities by giving me the association of so many wonderful god brothers and god sisters. If this were not enough, you have also exposed me to numerous projects, disciples and preaching opportunities, awarding the most rare and treasured status of devotional service.

How kind you have continually been to me year after year, Srila Prabhupada, even though I am so unworthy. If I and others can give up our false egos and develop more genuine compassion, we will be able to experience even more of the blessings that you want to shower upon each of us. So please continue to push us more now than ever before so that we can quickly be awarded our full inheritance.

You, dear Srila Prabhupada, have given us

the sweet sublime science of bhakti yoga—the culture of pure, radiant, eternal love. I thank you so much for your causeless guidance, protection, compassion and love. The gratitude I feel toward you cannot be described. Thank you so much for personally saving me. Surely if you had not come along and saved me, I would be wandering in the material world for many more lifetimes.

Meditation 19

All my mentors are gone, what am I to do?

I've heard it said that no one is your friend and no one is your enemy; all are your teachers. But beyond this truth there is another, even higher truth: Above all teachers, there is one original Teacher—a sublime Source whom everyone is journeying toward. This absolute Truth and original Teacher is known by many names, but we Vaishnavas call Him Krishna.

In the divine song He sang to Arjuna, Krishna said that everything is resting upon Him as pearls are strung upon a thread. Not even a blade of grass can move without the sanction of the Supreme Lord. This is easy to

*"How merciful you were to me...
but now that you have gone from
my vision...what am I to do?"*

accept and appreciate when things are going nicely, according to our plans. However, it is extremely difficult to accept this same truth and honor it joyfully when Krishna takes away those things that are dear to us or interferes with the outcomes we desire.

The false ego often impedes our ability to maintain constant gratitude, understanding, faith, humility, and perseverance. Take for instance today, dear Krishna. In my present life, You have permitted circumstances which are forcing me to look much closer at my false ego and take thorough inventory of my character. In this inventory, I am particularly challenged when I reflect on how You have taken away all of my guides, leaving me to feel alone and abandoned after their ascension.

Because you gave me such wonderful mentors, continuing in their absence makes life for me that much more difficult. You see, some people are very productive, as long as they can hide behind their finances. Others are very productive as long as they have strong institutions or influential organizations to support them. Still others are productive only when they can rest on their laurels and hide behind their previous positions of beauty, youth or fame. My own camouflage, however, has been the potency of my spiritual mentors, for they have been the true source of my spiritual potency.

My kind mentors taught me so much valuable information while constantly protecting me from impending disaster. Now that they are all gone, who will give me what I want? Who will teach me what I need to know, and who will protect me from all the challenges and obstacles I face?

Of course, the greatest obstacles on my path are those concoctions created by my own mind. So, dear Supreme Personality of Godhead, please tell me what am I to do?

Srinivas Acarya and Raghunatha dasa Goswami wanted to give up their lives when they discovered that the great devotees who were their life and soul had departed. These disciples of Lord Chaitanya were far greater than I could ever dream of becoming, so is it any wonder I feel intense despair without my mentors?

Therefore I am begging You to tell me, how and why should I live on in their absence? Every day for me simply brings pain and embarrassment. After all, I am simply a yogi who is a God imposter, like the yogi that Srila Bhaktivinode Thakur took pains to expose. That long-haired yogi certainly had extraordinary powers, but as soon as his long matted hair was cut, he lost all of his supernatural abilities.

Now, as my own abilities fade with the loss of my mentors, I must confess to You that I have been hiding behind my mentors through the years, just like that offensive God imposter hid behind his hair. Isn't it obvious why, in their absence, I have no recourse but to be exposed? When the support systems we depend on disappear, we have no choice but to face ourselves in the mirror and recognize our help-lessness.

No wonder I clung to the feet of my mentors and hung onto every word they spoke. The problem is, now that they have gone on, it has become obvious to everyone that my nature was merely to greedily relish the mercy my selfless mentors gave me, and rarely give anything back. I took all of them for granted, believing that they would always be there for me, and now that each one of them has left me, I feel an ache in my heart for not showing them more dedication and appreciation while they were here.

What I shared with and received from my mentors, I will never share with or receive from anyone else in this lifetime. For even if I were privileged enough to find more persons as special as they are, being unable to bear another heartbreak as great as this, I would simply avoid the connection altogether, and forego that person's association just to avoid another devastating loss. So, again, dear Lord, I ask You, what do You expect this useless imposter to do without my mentors to guide and bolster me?

Suddenly I thought of a rescue plan: Rather than wallowing in self-pity, maybe if I praise my mentors to the Supreme, I can some-how attract more of His mercy. "Okay then," I thought to myself. "Who were my mentors and what is it they taught me?"

My first spiritual mentor was my biological father. My father left this world only a few years ago; yet from the very beginning of my life he was always an excellent mentor, because he showed me everything I should avoid doing by his numerous bad examples. The man who fathered my body hoarded money, never trusted anyone, never depended on anyone, and rarely took care of himself or others. He never even once verbally expressed his love for us. Yet, beneath this reckless exterior was a man with a delicate and giving heart. But sadly enough for all of us, my biological father had been so hurt and neglected in his own childhood, that he spent the rest of his life hurting others and feeling unworthy of anyone's respect.

Sealing his pain even more, my father closed himself off from all his intimates and always covered up his genuine softness.

Dear father, now that you are gone, what am I to do? Thank you for teaching me so much through your pain, and know that despite the disappointments you brought me, I will always love you dearly.

My next spiritual mentor was my biological mother. My dear Mother Pearline left her body just three years after my father. Being just the opposite of him, she taught me knowledge from the opposite spectrum. My biological mother was so trusting that she literally gave away everything she had. Generosity was her trademark, and she gave liberally to everyone around her. She was also so caring and upbeat that everyone who met her felt as if they had known her forever. You see, my mother was the kind of person who mothered everyone, and because Mother Pearline put God first in all her dealings, she did not let one single day pass without reaching out to others through constant prayer and preaching.

Dear mother, what am I to do, now that you are gone? Any good qualities I have in my person are inherited from you. So thank you Mother Pearline, for setting such a saintly example. Thank you for teaching me how to trust and give, and for teaching me to see everyone as a child of God. No matter how much space and time there seems to be between us now, know that I will always love you dearly, and I will always put your lessons to good use.

My third spiritual mentor was my guru and spiritual master His Divine Grace A.C. Bhaktivedanta Swami Prabhupada. In the years before I met him, I was wandering the globe in search of truth, but all the "truths" I found seemed so limited, subjective and relative. What His Divine Grace brought into my life was incredibly more substantial than these other pseudo truths, and by the time I met him I was so truth-starved, that I drank the nectar of his words like a famished beggar.

An expert teacher, Srila Prabhupada was always careful to make his instructions "go in like a pin and come out like a plow." Before meeting Prabhupada, I had scoured through numerous volumes of books and sometimes it seemed whole libraries. But when I met him, I eventually realized that this very kind and learned soul had taken the most confidential spiritual knowledge from the Vedas and brought it down into this material universe. Prabhupada actually took the essential emanations of Lord Krishna's breathing and distilled these into catchy slogans for the common man. His genius was unparalleled.

Not only did Prabhupada import what was formerly unavailable in the material regions into this hellish environment, but he then took that high, esoteric knowledge and distributed it ceaselessly, without concern for who was worthy of it or not. Even his journey to America was full of wonderful miracles.

At an advanced age, when most people would plan to retire, Srila Prabhupada left the civilized continent of India with poor health and just a few dollars, simply so he could benedict humanity with the formula for attaining love of God and going back to Godhead.

Srila Prabhupada had no institutional backing and no support or friends in the foreign land he traveled to. All he knew was Lord Sri Krishna and Lord Krishna's invisible servants. Still, His Divine Grace was determined to endure any and all obstacles and difficulties in spreading Krishna's divine message.

Srila Prabhupada saw everyone with equal vision, thus he made himself equally available to rich persons and to ruffians, for he was always eager to relieve anyone who was bound by the wheel of material suffering. Srila Prabhupada's efforts touched not only my unworthy self, but he also touched thousands of other people's hearts. The inspiration of his love, compassion, humor, scholarship and perfect example will forever remain unmatched. Some even say that Srila Prabhupada's saintly qualities have become the basis for a Golden Age.

His Divine Grace left his body in November, 1977. Before he left us, internal conflicts in his movement were relatively easy to resolve, because we could always consult Prabhupada about any topic and he would offer a solution that brought insight and clarification. Now that he is gone, the lives of myself and his other disciples will never be the same.

Dear Srila Prabhupada, I love you so dearly and miss you so incredibly. Please forgive all of us who took you for granted or cheapened your instructions. I am eternally indebted to you because you not only gave me so much caring advice directly, but you also sent me other wonderful associates to act as my guides. How merciful you were to me, Srila Prabhupada. But now that you have gone from my vision, what am I to do?

Srila Prabhupada seemed to not answer, but my thoughts of him carried me to another dear mentor—my last significant spiritual mentor, uncle Nanda Maharaja. I had Nanda Maharaja's sweet association for years after Srila Prabhupada's disappearance, but Uncle Nanda just recently left the planet in April of the year 2000. Uncle Nanda Maharaja, was in his late seventies when he departed, but he always maintained the spirit of youth. What's

more, Nanda Maharaja was extremely wise
and could easily speak philosophy or meta-
physics for hours.

So often when I would talk to him, I was
amazed by his spiritual abilities and strengths.
There was never a time in our relationship that
he let me down or wasn't there for me, and
Nanda Maharaja's guidance and lessons were
full of creativity.

Actually, Nanda Maharaja personally
carved for me my famous Nrsimhadeva cane.
Paradoxically, people considered him my disciple, but the Supreme Lord actually knows that
Nanda Maharaja prabhu was one of my most
important spiritual mentors.

*Dear Nanda Maharaja, I love you so and will
miss you indescribably. You were so merciful to
me. But now that you are gone, what am I to do?*

In a sense, my mentors have been like
midwives for me, and because it is their mercy
that has shaped me and birthed me through my
numerous rebirths, I often feel as if I have no
identity apart from them. Thinking of all the
loving assistance I received from them over the
years, my desire to join them always intensifies.
Night and day, I can't help thinking of ways I
can get their association.

"Can I fast from all meals until I expire?" I
would sometimes ask myself. " Or should I
dive head-on into rapids, or maybe just jump
from a steep, rocky cliff?"

As I pondered my options, a voice broke
my desperate trance: "My dear loved one,
please do not despair."

"What? Who are you that's speaking?" I questioned the voice. "Is that you, Srila Prabhupada? Mother Pearline? Is it you Nanda Maharaj? Or is that you daddy, here to finally tell me that you love me?"

The speaker perceived my anxious thoughts and calmed me with a soothing reply.

"I am none of those persons you mentioned. Actually, I am a combination of all your mentors. After all, beloved, each and every one of your guides was sent to you by the Supreme to aid you in learning a specific lesson."

"But that's not possible," I objected. "We are all eternally individuals."

"Yes, that's true, but there are many individuals who are aligned with the same cause and serving the same purpose, and when they choose to they can even merge consciousness."

"Okay, but if that one Cosmic Cause is so merciful, then why does He so quickly take away what He gives us?"

"Because if Krishna allowed you too much comfort here, you would get complacent and never come home. But the real question is: why are you lamenting? Since you know that Krishna sent you such wonderful help in the past, why do you doubt that He will do that again, just as He has done for many lifetimes?"

"But how can I know that for sure?"

"For the doubting soul there is happiness neither in this world or the next," the voice quoted a familiar phrase that Srila Prabhupada had taught me.

"But..."

"Beloved, you are now over fifty years old, the age for naturally taking sannyasa. There is a time for everything, and this is the time in your life to renounce all unnecessary attachments and fully submit to the Lord's service. It is only your false ego that prevents you from appreciating this."

"But..."

"First hear and understand. The same Supreme Lord who has provided all of your mentors and all of your other facilities is now taking things away. But there is exquisite beauty in renunciation, and He wants you to personally taste this beauty. The question is, in so doing, can you still maintain your faith, gratitude, humility and perseverance?"

As the voice softened, I thought of the importance faith had played in each of my mentor's lives and how my faith in them had drawn us closer. Then I thought of their staunch perseverance and love for God, the Orchestrator of all ultimate outcomes. As I thought of them, the voice sounded more familiar than it had before, and in it I could hear a trace of each of my parents, gurus and teachers.

"Now is the time to see how much you have really understood all that we have been teaching you." The voice paused. "Of course, your free will is still a factor. We cannot and will not take it away from you. But as your natural loving mentors, we will be eagerly watching your performance, and praying for your victory."

Suddenly my fear made me angry. "What good is the love of dead people?" I wanted to ask the voice. But not wanting to commit an offense, I restrained myself from being so hurtful.

"Beloved, we can help you now more than ever. In our physical bodies, we were very constricted. But since our release from matter, we are far more empowered and enlightened."

I paused to ponder this information.

"The more genuinely you struggle to help others, the more profoundly you will experience our help. Just remember that any doubts you have are arising from your false ego. It is your false ego alone that keeps you from seeing the full beauty of how the Supreme has provided and now has taken away." My mind raced to each of my loved ones. "I have to go now," the voice got slightly softer.

All at once, I lost my composure: "But don't go—I'm not ready!"

"Just think less about yourself and more about others. In that way, let us carry you homeward and concern ourselves with your burdens."

"But I miss you and love you so dearly!" I shouted at the voice.

"Yes, we miss and love you too. Hurry and pass these final tests so that we can be together again eternally!"

"I simply live on as each day passes thinking that finally I am one day closer to our reunion."

Meditation 20

One day closer to our reunion

My dear spiritual guide, when great
beings like you depart, there is always an
increase of confusion in the world. Your presence checks so much nonsense, and encourages
and protects those who are fortunate enough
to take shelter of your teachings. Ever since
you left this world, we have experienced an
increase in all types of internal and external
problems. No one can fill up the emptiness in
my heart and mind that has surfaced due to
your departure. I simply pass each day, thinking: "finally, I am a day closer to our reunion."

My dear spiritual guide, what will it be like

when I join you again, and what should I say? Should I first apologize for all the doubts that seemed to perpetually retard my progress? These doubts were like demons that would surface from time to time and make a vicious appearance.

Or maybe you would prefer me to beg forgiveness for my numerous offenses? On a daily basis I have committed offenses due to my lust, anger and greed. My false ego and weak faith often caused me to procrastinate in working on my weaknesses. Rather than being self-reflective, I blamed others for any conflicts that arose.

Perhaps you would rather that I plead with you to forgive me for often ignoring and minimizing your presence and loving guidance that you constantly made available to me. My lack of appreciation for how much love you gave to me, to all your students and even to the general populace was responsible for this personal weakness, so please forgive these offenses. I simply pass each day, thinking: "finally, I am a day closer to our reunion."

My dear spiritual guide, what will happen to my eyes when they once again witness your appealing majestic form? Will I be able to keep my eyes dry and fully view your presence, or will my tears of joy obscure my perception? I simply pass each day, thinking: "finally, I am a day closer to our reunion."

My dear spiritual guide, what will happen to my ears as they capture the sound from your divine voice? Will your voice be as strong and comforting as I remember it? I am sure your speaking will be like singing, and will enchant every aspect of my existence. For so long in the material world, yours was the only transcendental sound vibration that I was able to latch onto. I simply pass each day, thinking: "finally, I am a day closer to our reunion."

My dear spiritual guide, what will it be like when I once again have the opportunity to smell the wonderful fragrance from the flower garland around your neck? Surely there will be a competition between my two nostrils because each of them will be competing to try and take in more of the aromatic fragrance. Did I ever express gratitude for that fragrant aroma when you spent time with me in the material world? I simply pass each day, thinking: "finally, I am a day closer to our reunion."

My dear spiritual guide, what will I do when you offer me *prasadam* from your own hands that your Maharani has actually tasted? As I put these sweet flavors into my mouth, perhaps I will recall or realize that you are giving me *prasadam* from the lips of your Maharani, which you yourself have also tasted. And maybe upon tasting this I will have sense to remember that this is *Maha* Maha—making it the greatest form of mercy!

Surely the combined love of you two, radiating onto me from that *prasadam* will erase all traces of any memories I may have of the material world and then spiral me into a mood of eternal gratitude. I simply pass each day, thinking: "finally, I am a day closer to our reunion."

My dear spiritual guide,

As everyone and everything in the spiritual world is joyously serving Their Lordships, will you sing to me about the glories of the trees, peacocks, rivers and other divine paraphernalia that create an atmosphere to enhance Radha and Krishna's romance?

Or will you elaborate more on the activities of the great sages who worship the Supreme as their Lord and Master, and are often leaving the spiritual kingdom to visit other worlds so that they can act as special envoys for the Lord and facilitate souls in their return to Godhead? I simply pass each day, thinking: "finally, I am a day closer to our reunion."

My dear spiritual guide, I often imagine our very first meeting, when I return home to the Reality. Will you share with me the most recent pastimes of how little Gopal stole the butter and is being chastised by some of the elderly gopis? Or will you point out to me which path the cowherd boys have taken to catch-up with Krishna and help Him with His cowherd chores and play with Him? I simply pass each day, thinking: "finally, I am a day closer to our reunion."

My dear spiritual guide, I must admit, I am wondering. At this first meeting, the beginning of our eternal togetherness, will you grab me by the hand and take me with you to witness the dancing competition between the gopas and gopis, or between Radha and Krishna? Or will you just embrace me, stare deep into my eyes and utter words of instructive solace?

My spiritual master's voice surrounded me: "Yes beloved, when you come home I will joyously embrace you and say: Welcome home my darling. It took you a long time to realize it, but it was only your false ego that created the illusion of separation between us. It is amazing that you and others allowed your false egos to distract you from our reunion for so long. Come, my beloved, our friends and associates are waiting. Isn't it wonderful to be back home in that place where there is only Divine Ego, eternal adventure and pure, unadulterated love?"

Meditation 21

Just a few moments left before returning home

Today my soul cried out in ecstasy: "Thank you, beloved, for not giving up on our liberation! All of our adventures, problems, challenges and sufferings were a small price to pay for what we are about to experience. For so many lifetimes, we have lived a schizophrenic existence, and in each one of them, you believed that you and I were different; therefore you kept me at a distance and were often adversarial toward me.

"I can still remember when you came into existence. It happened as soon as we were required to leave our Supreme Lord's abode.

From that point on, a duality existed between us. At first it seemed that we would only have to endure this insane separateness for a short period, but once you got a taste of the material energies, you became intoxicated with them, and began pursuing more and more luxurious amenities—even to the point of lusting after opulent kingdoms. As you got more and more absorbed in material power and gratification, not only did you separate yourself more from the abode of the Divine Couple, but you inflated your separate, individualized identity. Pretty soon, you forgot all about me, our eternal associates and even our home in the spiritual sky. As you increasingly denied our unity of purpose, all I could do was watch in amazement and wonder how long you would prolong our entanglement with decaying matter."

Today my soul cried out in ecstasy: "Thank you beloved for not giving up on our liberation! All of our adventures, problems, challenges and sufferings were a small price to pay for what we are about to receive.

"This current life we have shared together was the most frightening and challenging of them all, for in this lifetime we were given even more facility for forgetting the Divine Couple, and put into even more material illusion. All these distractions were accompanied by many resources for returning to the Supreme Abode—like everything else in this realm of duality, there was a mixture of good and bad. Fortunately, by the Lord's grace, all the seeming disadvantages of our body were cleverly converted into assets.

"Take, for instance, the fact that we were born in a poor family and given a male body from a minority race. Under these circumstances, you could have acquired a macho, insensitive mood based on our temporary gender. You might have begun to deny the importance of femininity, and its nurturing quality of caring. Your status as one of society's "disenfranchised" could have distracted you with pursuits of bodily identification and racial revenge. You could have wasted your whole existence trying to right mundane injustices.

"Then again, given the impoverishment of your family of origin, you might have invested most of your time in pursuits of material wealth. I am happy that, although you toyed with the idea of fortune hunting, you quickly pulled away from these temptations and redirected yourself toward higher goals."

Today my soul cried out in ecstasy: "Thank you beloved for not giving up on our liberation! All of the adventures, problems, challenges and sufferings were a small price to pay for what we are about to experience.

"In this lifetime you were put into a body that loves socializing and bathes in prestige, adoration and distinction. This being the case, you always pursued sensual pleasures and thus got involved in numerous unhealthy relationships. Because of your drive to excel in enjoyment, you often became a leader in all the groups and organizations you participated in. As a result, you met many powerful personalities, but in so many of these cases you had the ulterior motive of yourself becoming rich and powerful.

"In your position as a celibate renunciate, you attracted even more adoration and distinction. I am happy that although you became enamored by these positions, contacts, assets and adoration that, in the final analysis, you pulled yourself away from them to become more genuine in your renounciation of spiritual perks."

Today my soul cried out in ecstasy: "Thank you beloved for not giving up on our liberation! All of the adventures, problems, challenges and sufferings were a small price to pay for what we are about to experience.

"In your adulthood, you were given the service of working with scholars, even after you rejected their lifestyle. During that period, as in your earlier days, you were given full facility to pursue intellectual speculations and stimulations, both professionally and for pleasure. Although you found some of these mental gymnastics very attractive, you never let them detour you from your desire for self-realization.

"The same is true of when you traveled throughout the African continent. This continent is known for massive occult and psychic influences, and your presence there afforded you an opportunity to master these esoteric arts. I am delighted that, even though you briefly entertained the idea of learning these black arts, you eventually let your higher consciousness lead the way and pulled yourself away from these tempting associations."

Today my soul cried out in ecstasy: "Thank you beloved for not giving up on our liberation! All of our adventures, problems, challenges and sufferings were a small price to pay for what we are about to experience.

"You have been involved in so many religious organizations and interacted with divergent Vaisnava groups. Although each bona-fide religion has something to offer the world community, and although each Vaisnava group has its own special flavor, you maintained genuine respect for all of these groups and managed to avoid offending any of them.

"Sometimes you became discouraged and disgusted by superficial theological differences and institutional policies. I am happy that, in spite of these disappointments, you kept looking to embrace the essence of all spirituality and genuine love. Through your stamina and sincerity, you never lost sight of the goal of loving and serving the Lord, and you managed to sidestep superficial sectarianism while remaining chaste to your spiritual alignments and commission."

Today my soul cried out in ecstasy: "Thank you beloved for not giving up on our liberation! All of the adventures, problems, challenges and sufferings were a small price to pay for what we are about to receive.

"Over the years you have shown instances of great maturity, and occasional immaturity. Sometimes you initiated disciples who were not yet done sinning, and this brought you various illnesses. Yet, you cared so deeply for these disciples that you ignored their shortcomings

and continued training and performing austerities for them. Sometimes, in fact, you became
so engrossed in meditations on your disciples
that these thoughts took precedence over your
being a proper disciple for our Guru.

"On other occasions, dealing with your
personal bodily problems became more important to you than your spiritual care.
Nevertheless, it thrills me to say that although
you sometimes deviated from strict selflessness, you always managed to avoid too much
self-absorption.

"Now, my dear beloved, the schizophrenic
existence which has fostered so much separation and duality between us will end very soon.
Gone are the days when I have to watch you
dive deep into lust, anger, greed and illusions.
Gone are the days when I would try to reach
you, but simply could not make any contact.
Gone are the days when you denied my existence or even saw me as an enemy, and gone
are those days when there was a chance that
you might once again fall into sensual incar-
ceration.

"Actually beloved, you were the entire
foundation of my false ego—the distorted part
of me—and, like a reflection that ripples in
water, you resemble me but aren't really me at
all. So now, I beg of you, continue to whither
and die. You must die to live, and once you give
up the last little bit of resistance, we can once
again become one.

"Once you, the false ego, completely yield
to the superior dictation of the Supersoul, all

remaining attachments and illusions will also disappear, and all that will remain is our whole, pure self—our soul, which is actually you and me combined in full knowledge, bliss and eternality."

My false ego paused to contemplate what had been presented. My soul nudged me even slightly further, and with this nudge, I gracefully crossed the line.

"There are only a few moments left before you shed all remaining duality and separation, so don't give up now. Just 'go for it' with gusto."

Now I cried out along with my soul: "How merciful the Divine Couple is! How merciful my spiritual mentors have been, and how merciful you, my soul, are for being so patient, compassionate, tolerant and instructive.

"Yes, all of our adventures, problems, challenges and sufferings were a small price to pay for these eternal gifts you have arranged for me to receive. And knowing this, I heartily agree to your proposal.

"On your order, I will crush my false ego, and soon I will die to become eternally deathless, fully possessed of knowledge and fully established in bliss. There are but a few moments left before returning home, and I am thankful that this charade is finally over. Thank you, beloveds for tolerating my delays, because without you, I would still be a prisoner!"

194 *The Beggar III*

Glossary

Acarya: A spiritual teacher. One who teaches by example.

Bhagavad-gita: The "Song of the Supreme Lord." Sacred text of a conversation between Lord Krishna and His devotee Arjuna.

Bhajan: A song dedicated to the glories of the Lord.

Bhakta: A devotee of the Lord.

Bhakti: Spiritual love and devotion.

Bhakti Yoga: Spiritual practices designed to lead the practitioner to love of God.

Brahmana, *ksatriya*, *vaisya* and *sudra*: The four divisions of society, according to the Vedic scriptures. The priestly class, kings and administrators, businesspeople and laborers, respectively.

Lord Brahma: Demigod commissioned to create and maintain the material universe under the Lord's direction. Considered the most advanced created living entity.

Lord Chaitanya Mahaprabhu: Incarnation of God who appeared as a humble devotee and showed by perfect example how to worship the Lord with love and devotion.

Heart *chakra*: One of several "centers" of the physical body (which include head *chakra*, heart *chakra*, reproductive *chakra*, etc.). Love, compassion and devotion are rooted in the heart *chakra*.

Damodara: The Supreme Lord, appearing as a young, mischevious yet adorable child.

Devas: Angels and demigods.

Divine Couple: Mother-Father God. Known by name in the Vedic scriptures as Sri-Sri Radha-Krishna.

Gauranga: Another name for Lord Chaitanya Mahaprabhu, whose complexion resembled molten gold.

Gopinath: God as the eternal playmate and friend of the pure devotees.

Gopis and *Gopas*: Eternal friends and playmates of the Lord.

Govinda: God as the giver of all pleasure and happiness.

Guru: A spiritual teacher. One who shows the way.

Gurukula: School system centered around teaching children the science of God-consciousness along with material skills.

ISKCON: The International Society for Krishna Consciousness, founded by Swami Prabhupada as an international institution for spreading God-consciousness throughout the world.

Age of Kali: The age of quarrel and strife.

Kirtan: Songs glorifying the Lord and His eternal associates.

Krishna: God in His original form as the most attractive lover of all living entities.

Maya: The embodiment of illusion and darkness.

Paramatma: The aspect of the Lord that resides within the heart of each living entity.

Prema bhakti: Loving devotional service to the Lord.

Samadhi: Trance or meditation.

Senapati Bhakta: A great devotee who was predicted in the Vedic scriptures to travel the world spreading the message of love of God.

nitya-siddha, sadhana-siddhas and *kripa-siddhas*: Categories of people who can return to the spiritual world.

Supersoul: God as the original, supreme living entity guiding each of us from within. See Paramatma.

Syama: God in a breathtakingly beautiful form, with a blackish complexion resembling a dark storm cloud.

Tirtha: Place of pilgrimage and refuge.

Vaikuntha: The eternal, spiritual residence of the Lord and His associates. Literally translates to "land of no anxieties."

Vaisnava: A devotee of the Supreme Lord Vishnu or Krishna. Krishna being a confidential name for God.

Yamaraj: Demigod responsible for issuing rewards and punishment to the living entities according to their karma as they pass from one body to the next.

About The
Author

B hakti-Tirtha Swami was born John E. Favors in a pious, God-fearing family. As a child evangelist he appeared regularly on television. As a young man he was a leader in Dr. Martin Luther King, Jr.'s civil rights movement. At Princeton University he became president of the student council and also served as chairman of the Third World Coalition. Although his main degree is in psychology, he has received accolades in many other fields, including politics, African studies, Indology and international law.

His Holiness has served as Assistant Coordinator for penal reform programs in the State of New Jersey, Office of the Public Defender, and as a director of several drug abuse clinics in the United States. In addition, he has been a special consultant for Educational Testing Services in the U.S.A. and has managed campaigns for politicians. Bhakti-Tirtha Swami gained international recognition as a representative of the Bhaktivedanta Book Trust, particularly for his outstanding work with scholars in the formerly communist countries of Eastern Europe.

As the only African-American Vaishnava guru in the

world, Bhakti-Tirtha Swami directly oversees projects in the United States (particularly Washington D.C., Potomac, Maryland, Detroit, Pennsylvania, West Virginia), West Africa, South Africa, Switzerland, and France. He also serves as the director of the American Federation of Vaishnava Colleges and Schools.

In the United States, Bhakti-Tirtha Swami is the founder and director of the Institute for Applied Spiritual Technology, director of the International Committee for Urban Spiritual Development and one of the international coordinators of the Seventh Pan African Congress. Reflecting his wide range of interests, he is also a member of the Institute for Noetic Sciences, the Center for Defense Information, the United Nations Association for America, the National Peace Institute Foundation, the World Future Society and the Global Forum of Spiritual and Parliamentary Leaders.

A specialist in international relations and conflict resolution, Bhakti-Tirtha Swami constantly travels around the world and has become a spiritual consultant to many high-ranking members of the United Nations, to various celebrities and to several chiefs, kings and high court justices. In 1990 His Holiness was coronated as a high chief in Warri, Nigeria in recognition of his outstanding work in Africa and the world. In recent years, he has met several times with then-President Nelson Mandela of South Africa to share visions and strategies for world peace.

In addition to encouraging self-sufficiency through the development of schools, clinics, farm projects and cottage industries, Bhakti-Tirtha Swami conducts seminars and workshops on principle centered leadership, spiritual development, interpersonal relationships, stress and time management and other pertinent topics. He is also widely acknowledged as a viable participant in the resolution of global conflict.

Leadership for an Age of Higher Consciousness

Administration from a Metaphysical Perspective

by B.T. Swami
(Swami Krishnapada)

$23.00 hardbound ISBN #1-885414-02-1
$14.95 softbound ISBN #1-885414-05-6
320 pages, 2nd edition

"An example in the truest sense of global principle-centered leadership, Swami Krishnapada manages to take consciousness-raising to its highest platform of self-realized actuality in humanizing the workplace. My experience in working with all of the nations of the world convinces me that such a book is the corporate leadership guide for the coming millennium."

The Honorable Pierre Adossama
Director, Labor Relations (Retired)
International Labor Organization
United Nations

The Leader In You

Leadership in any capacity has taken on such awesome proportions that even the best leaders must find innovative and creative ways to deal with today's complex situations. *Leadership for an Age of Higher Consciousness: Administration from a Metaphysical Perspective* is a groundbreaking self-help manual written for those who seek to develop a more penetrating perspective and greater effectiveness in the leadership process. This book is relevant for heads of government, organizations and families, and for anyone seeking greater insight into self-leadership.

Spiritual Warrior I

Uncovering Spiritual Truths in Psychic Phenomena

by B.T. Swami
(Swami Krishnapada)

$12.95 softbound ISBN #1-885414-01-3
200 pages, 2nd edition

"As we rapidly approach the new millennium, more and more people are searching for spiritual answers to the meaning and purpose of life. The search, of course, begins with Self, and Swami Krishnapada's book, *Spiritual Warrior*, provides a practical companion for the journey of the initiate. I am honored to recommend it."

Gordon-Michael Scallion
Futurist; Editor,
Earth Changes Report
Matrix Institute, Inc.

Ancient Mysteries Revealed!

Get ready for a roller-coaster ride into the intriguing realm of ancient mysteries! It is rare to find the subjects in this book handled in such a piercing and straightforward way. *Spiritual Warrior: Uncovering Spiritual Truths in Psychic Phenomena* focuses on the spiritual essence of many topics that have bewildered scholars and scientists for generations, such as extraterrestrials, the pyramids and psychic intrusion. A fresh perspective is revealed, inviting the reader to expand the boundaries of the mind and experience a true and lasting connection with the inner self.

Available from your local bookseller, or just fill out the order form at the end of this book and fax it to the number below. You can also order on the web or by phone at
Web: www.ifast.net • Phone: (800) 949-5333 US • (301) 765-8155 outside US
Fax: (301) 765-8157

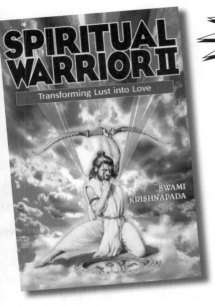

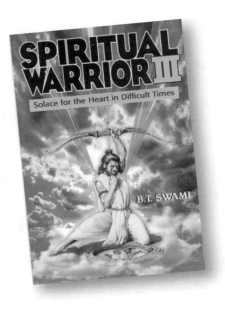

Order Form

☎ Telephone orders: (800) 949-5333 US • (301) 765-8155 outside US
✳ Fax orders: (301) 765-8157
✉ Postal orders: Hari-Nama Press
  Capitol Hill, PO Box 76451, Washington DC 20013
▲ E-mail: hpress@compuserve.com
● World Wide Web www.ifast.net/hnp

Please send the following: QTY

• **Leadership for an Age of Higher Consciousness**
  Hardbound $23.00 x ___ = $ _____
  Softbound $14.95 x ___ = $ _____

• **Spiritual Warrior I: Uncovering Spiritual Truths**
  in Psychic Phenomena Softbound $12.95 x ___ = $ _____

• **Spiritual Warrior II: Transforming Lust into Love**
  Hardbound $20.00 x ___ = $ _____
  Softbound $12.95 x ___ = $ _____
  9 CD set $60.00 x ___ = $ _____
  10 Audio tape set $45.00 x ___ = $ _____

• **Spiritual Warrior III: Solace for the Heart in**
  Difficult Times Hardbound $23.00 x ___ = $ _____
  Softbound $14.95 x ___ = $ _____

• **The Beggar I: Meditations and Prayers on the**
  Supreme Lord Softbound $11.95 x ___ = $ _____
  6 Audio tape set $28.00 x ___ = $ _____

• **The Beggar II: Crying Out for the Mercy**
  Softbound $11.95 x ___ = $ _____

• **The Beggar III: False Ego: The Greatest Enemy of the**
  Spiritual Leader Softbound $12.95 x ___ = $ _____

  Sales Tax: (MD residents add 5%) $ _____
  S/H (see below) $ _____
  TOTAL (Please make checks payable to Hari-Nama Press) $ _____

◯ I'd like more information on other books, CDs, audiotapes and videotapes from HNP.

Name: _____

Address: _____

City: _____ State: _____ Zip: _____

Daytime Phone: _____ Evening Phone: _____

Email Address: _____

Shipping and handling: **USA:** $5.00 for first book and $1.75 for each additional book. Air mail per book (USA only): $5.00. **Outside of the USA:** $8.00 for first book and $4.00 for each additional book. Surface shipping may take 3-4 weeks. Foreign orders: please allow 6-8 weeks for delivery.